Discovering
The Love of Your Life

LEONARDO TAVARES

Discovering
The Love of Your Life

DISCOVERING THE LOVE OF YOUR LIFE

May this book be an embrace,
A solace to your weary soul,
May it instill confidence
That the odyssey to self-love
Can be embarked upon with authenticity.

No pursuit is insurmountable,
For the connection we share with our being
Transcends tribulations, surpasses trials,
Becoming an eternal fountain
Of self-discovery and evolution.

May your uncertainty transform into confidence,
And let experiences be treasures,
May your insecurities dissolve into nothing,
And may the light illuminate the path
Of those in quest of advancement.

This book is a celebration,
For all who have undertaken the voyage of self-adoration,
And for those seizing the prospect of growth,
May it be a sanctuary of inspiration and empowerment.

And in the throes of most arduous moments,
May we summon fortitude and resolve
To progress onward, to embrace the present,
The lessons learned, and to lead our lives
With self-regard, acceptance, and resilience.

CONTENTS

FOREWORD

In the midst of the whirlwind of life, we often find ourselves in pursuit of something that seems out of reach. It can be easy to get lost in the maelstrom of external expectations, the fleeting promises of fairy tales, and the never-ending quest for love that we all too often neglect to direct towards the most important person in our lives: ourselves.

"Discovering the Love of Your Life" is more than just a book; it is an odyssey of self-discovery and acceptance. As you journey through the pages of this tome, you will be guided on a profound exploration of the most foundational relationship you can have: the one with yourself.

Every chapter is filled with wisdom, revelations, and tools for nurturing a loving connection with your very being. So be prepared to embark on each page with an open mind and heart, for the journey to self-love is a courageous and transformative choice. No matter where you are on your path, know that the quest for the love of your life begins and ends within you.

With love and gratitude,

Leonardo Tavares

CHAPTER 1

INTRODUCTION

Blossom like the love that seeks,
the most precious garden is the one
you tend within yourself.

"To love another, you must first love yourself." These words are often quoted, but we rarely stop to consider their profound meaning. Imagine yourself as a garden: your flowers represent your relationships with others, and the butterflies that grace them represent shared experiences. Now, think about the soil in which this garden grows – that soil is your self-love. If the soil is rich and cared for, your flowers will bloom beautifully, attracting butterflies that are equally resplendent. But if the soil is depleted and neglected, your flowers will wither and attract butterflies that bring them no beauty.

Welcome to a transformative journey towards self-love and healthy relationships. In Discovering the Love of Your Life, we will embark together on a profound and momentous odyssey that will revolutionize how you perceive, value, and connect with others. Throughout the following pages, we will dive into the seas of self-esteem, self-acceptance, and self-discovery. Prepare to forge an authentic connection with yourself and to establish strong foundations for relationships that are in harmony with your true essence.

THE SIGNIFICANCE OF SELF-LOVE
FOR HEALTHY RELATIONSHIPS

In a world that often bombards us with idealized depictions of romance and fairy tales, it's easy to overlook a fundamental aspect of any lasting and meaningful relationship: self-love. Before embarking on a romantic journey with another soul, it's crucial that we first master the art of cherishing ourselves wholeheartedly and unconditionally. This opus, Discovering the Love of Your Life, serves as a compass for navigating the turbulent waters of relationships, anchored in the bedrock of self-love.

Imagine a magnificent building. No matter how grand its superstructure, if its foundation is weak, it is doomed to collapse. Similarly, our relationships are built on a foundation of self-love. We often enter into relationships with the expectation that the other person will fill our voids, make us whole, and give us the happiness we seek. However, this approach places an unfair burden on both partners.

Self-love is not egotism; rather, it is the cornerstone of a balanced life and healthy relationships. When we have genuine self-respect, we are able to share our love authentically without the expectation of external fulfillment. This allows us to build relationships based on partnership, mutual respect, and shared growth. Self-love empowers us to set healthy boundaries, communicate our needs, and make decisions that are in our best long-term interests.

HOW THIS BOOK WILL TRANSFORM YOUR LOVE ODYSSEY

The journey of finding and nurturing self-love can seem daunting at first. Many of us have been conditioned to believe that taking care of ourselves is selfish, or that we need validation from others to see our own worth. But I assure you, you are worthy of love and deserving of feeling complete just as you are.

This book is a compassionate guide to accompany you on your voyage of self-discovery and personal growth. Every page, every chapter, has been carefully crafted to offer insights, practical strategies, and authentic anecdotes from people who have transformed their lives by prioritizing self-love. Here, you will find a safe space to explore your beliefs, overcome obstacles, and embrace the unique beauty that resides within you.

Preparing for the Odyssey

Before we set out, I invite you to open yourself to the possibility of growth and transformation. This book requires commitment and authenticity on your part. I am here to encourage and guide you, but it is you who will make the choices and take the steps necessary for your own evolution.

Throughout this journey, be gentle with yourself. Self-love is not a race; it is an ongoing journey of learning and growth. Be open to challenging limiting beliefs, embracing your vulnerabilities, and celebrating your victories, no matter how small they may seem.

Know that this is an ongoing process. Just as plants need water and sunlight to thrive, you must regularly nurture your self-love. The goal of this book is not to provide instant solutions, but to equip you with the tools and insights you need to walk the path of self-discovery and self-acceptance.

Each page you turn will bring you closer to a profound understanding of who you are and the love you deserve to receive. Know that you are not alone. Together, we will travel the pathways of the heart and mind, and you will discover that you are more prepared than ever to foster healthy and loving relationships.

Are you ready to embark on this transformative odyssey towards self-love and the relationships you deserve? Then, turn the page and begin crafting a future filled with love, growth, and authenticity.

CHAPTER 2

UNVEILING SELF-LOVE

"To love oneself is the beginning
of a lifelong romance."
Oscar Wilde

The first step on the journey to finding the love of your life begins within yourself. Self-love is the foundation upon which all other relationships blossom. In this chapter, we will explore the core of self-love, plumbing its essence, elucidating its significance, and discerning its manifestations in our lives. We will also examine the tell-tale signs of low self-esteem and a lack of self-love, so you can become familiar with these harmful patterns.

DECIPHERING THE NOTION OF SELF-LOVE

Self-love is more than just a buzzword or a sunny affirmation we repeat to ourselves. It is an attitude, a relationship, and a profound commitment to oneself. Self-love is the foundation upon which respect and affection for one's own being can flourish, regardless of external circumstances. It extends beyond physical appearance to encompass inner attributes, accomplishments, and values.

Imagine yourself as your own best friend. Would you be willing to constantly criticize and belittle this friend? Of course not. Self-love is treating oneself with the same gentleness and compassion that one would extend to a beloved friend. It means acknowledging one's imperfections while also celebrating strengths and achievements. Self-love is an ongoing journey of self-discovery, acceptance, and growth, on which you become your own strongest advocate, constantly seeking what is best for your well-being.

DISCERNING SIGNS OF DIMINISHED SELF-STEEM AND LACK OF SELF-LOVE

Sometimes, it can be difficult to recognize the presence of low self-esteem or a lack of self-love in ourselves. Self-negativity can lurk beneath the surface and become an integral part of our thinking. The following are some indicative signs that you might be struggling with a lack of self-love:

Excessive Self-Criticism

Excessive self-criticism is like a fog that obscures our clear perception of ourselves. It is a cognitive pattern in which we tend to focus solely on our flaws and imperfections, while ignoring our accomplishments and positive qualities. Imagine having a friend who constantly points out your shortcomings and never celebrates your successes. This is how excessive self-criticism operates inwardly.

Oftentimes, self-criticism stems from patterns of unrealistic expectations or comparisons with others. If you frequently compare yourself to people who seem to have everything together, it can be easy to fall into the trap of criticizing yourself for not being as perfect as they seem. However, this comparison fails to take into account the full reality of each individual, which includes their own hidden struggles and challenges.

Excessive self-criticism can also stem from internalized criticisms that we have learned from past experiences. Perhaps, there were times when you were harshly criticized, and these experiences have shaped the way you talk to yourself internally. This critical voice can become so pervasive that even when you accomplish something noteworthy, it insists on pointing out what could have been better.

The Perpetual Pitfall of Comparison

The trap of perpetual comparison is one of the most challenging to escape, as it leads us into a spiral of self-deprecation and discontent. When we engage in negative comparisons with others, we are, in essence, comparing our behind-the-scenes to their spotlight moments. This detrimental habit thwarts the recognition of our own uniqueness and intrinsic worth.

The compulsion for constant comparison often stems from the quest for external validation. This can be due to societal or cultural pressure to conform to particular benchmarks of success, beauty, or accomplishment. As we observe others attaining these benchmarks, our self-esteem diminishes, as we feel inadequate by comparison.

The Problem with Comparison is that it is Rooted in an Illusion: The illusion that we have an all-encompassing understanding of another's life. In reality, we are glimpsing only a limited part of their story. The insecurities and challenges they grapple with are seldom visible on the surface.

Challenge in Embracing Compliments

Having difficulty embracing compliments is a telltale sign of low self-esteem and a lack of self-love. While it may seem like a simple reaction, it has profound implications for how you perceive yourself. When you struggle to internalize positive praise, you are effectively rejecting acknowledgment and validation of your own greatness.

This difficulty often stems from feeling undeserving of compliments or positive attention. It may be linked to deeply ingrained beliefs of inadequacy. At times, this belief is so potent that even when others attempt to highlight your qualities, you find ways to divert or downplay your accomplishments.

Refusing to accept compliments can have various adverse consequences. First, it hinders the cultivation of healthy relationships, as others may perceive that your sense of appreciation is not genuinely received. Second, this self-deprecating stance perpetuates low self-esteem, as it reinforces the notion that you are undeserving of positive recognition.

Craving for Approval

The relentless pursuit of approval is akin to an emotional addiction that ensnares you in a cycle of emotional dependency on others. This need arises when your sense of self-worth becomes intertwined with external opinions and expectations. Instead of relying on your own perception, you seek external validation to substantiate your worth.

The genesis of this need often lies in past experiences where you linked others' approval to a fleeting sense of acceptance and love. Perhaps you were conditionally praised or received affection and attention only when you met specific expectations. Consequently, your self-esteem became contingent on external endorsement.

This quest for approval has several detrimental implications. First, it burdens your relationships, as you are constantly seeking signs of validation. This can foster a pattern of unsatisfactory relationships, where your emotional needs are eclipsed by others' expectations.

Profound Perfectionism

The suffocating grip of extreme perfectionism can crush your self-esteem and erode your ability to enjoy life to the fullest. It is an unyielding pursuit of excellence in all areas, often accompanied by a constant sense of dissatisfaction and relentless self-demand. While striving for excellence can be a commendable trait, extreme perfectionism can be debilitating and harmful.

The roots of perfectionism often lie in a fear of failure and a never-ending quest for external validation. The ceaseless pursuit of flawlessness often stems from the belief that your self-worth hinges on flawless performance. This mindset puts you under constant pressure to meet unattainable standards, which may be self-imposed or imposed by external expectations.

Extreme perfectionists often lack self-compassion. Every mistake is magnified, and even successes fail to bring satisfaction. Additionally, this unyielding pursuit of perfection can lead to procrastination and avoidance of tasks, as the fear of falling short of self-imposed standards looms large.

Avoidance of Challenges

The practice of avoiding challenges due to the fear of failure is like living in a comfort zone, but this comfort zone can morph into an emotional prison. The trepidation of failure often stems from a desire to protect one's self-image and avoid validating one's insecurities.

The avoidance of challenges can have many negative consequences. First and foremost, it stunts personal and professional growth by preventing you from taking risks and exploring new opportunities. Additionally, by avoiding challenges, you miss the opportunity to learn from mistakes and build resilience, two essential pillars of growth.

The fear of failure often stems from the belief that failure confirms inadequacy or worthlessness. This can create a self-destructive cycle in which self-doubt takes root, leaving no room for trial and error, an essential part of any growth process.

Neglect of Self-Care

The disregard for self-care is a pattern that relegates you to the background, prioritizing the needs and desires of others at the expense of your own. While tending to others is a noble quality, consistent self-neglect can lead to physical, mental, and emotional exhaustion. It's like trying to fill the cups of others while your own cup remains empty.

The neglect of self-care often stems from a mindset that attending to oneself is selfish or indulgent. However, it's important to acknowledge that self-care isn't a luxury but rather a fundamental necessity to maintain a healthy equilibrium in all aspects of life.

By neglecting self-care, you run the risk of compromising your mental and physical well-being. It can also impact your self-esteem, as you're conveying to yourself that your own needs are unimportant. This can lead to feelings of resentment and depletion, resulting in a cycle of low self-esteem.

Toxic Relationships

Entering into or staying in toxic relationships is a common challenge that can have a profound impact on your self-esteem and emotional well-being. This happens when you remain in relationships that are harmful, disrespectful, or fundamentally unhealthy, often due to a fear of being alone or the uncertainty of the unknown.

The tendency to endure toxic relationships often stems from insecurities and low self-esteem. You may believe that you don't deserve better or that you won't find someone who truly accepts you. The prospect of loneliness can be daunting, and this fear can lead you to settle for less than you deserve.

The reality is that staying in a toxic relationship only perpetuates the cycle of low self-esteem. You may find yourself compromising your own values, boundaries, and needs to keep the relationship going.

Sense of Inner Emptiness

The sense of inner emptiness is a profound feeling of dissatisfaction and unfulfillment, even in the face of significant achievements in life. This emptiness can be unsettling, leading to contemplations about life's purpose and the essence of personal fulfillment. It's as if there exists an emotional void that remains untouched by external accomplishments.

This sentiment is often rooted in a disconnection from oneself and a lack of alignment with one's authentic values and desires. The ceaseless pursuit of external goals can result in a neglect of one's inner world and emotional needs.

The inner void can also be exacerbated by limiting beliefs that tie one's self-esteem to external accomplishments. One might find themselves caught in a perpetual cycle of validation-seeking and success-chasing, hoping that these achievements will satiate the emotional void.

Walking Towards Self-Love

Understanding the essence of self-love and recognizing the signs of diminished self-esteem are the foundation of your journey. In the next chapter, we will delve even deeper into the art of rebuilding your self-worth. You will learn how to challenge negative thoughts, embrace your vulnerabilities, and wholeheartedly embark on the journey of self-discovery.

Remember, self-love is an expedition, and we are only just beginning to explore the vast realm of your own being. With courage and openness, continue your journey, for the love you seek already resides within you, waiting to be revealed and nurtured.

CHAPTER 3

REBUILDING YOUR SELF-ESTEEM

As an architect of the heart,
strive to reconstruct your
self-esteem with self-love.

Self-esteem is the foundation of self-love, often shaped by our perception of our own imperfections. The act of rebuilding your self-esteem entails an experience of unconditional self-acceptance, in which you embrace all of your quirks and idiosyncrasies. In this chapter, we will embark on an exploration of how you can learn to cherish the unique individual that you are, while also providing practical exercises designed to help you nurture and strengthen your self-esteem.

EMBRACING IMPERFECTIONS AND EMBODYING INDIVIDUALITY

The journey towards rebuilding your self-esteem begins with the unwavering acceptance of who you are. This entails recognizing your imperfections, embracing your individuality, and loving yourself fully, with all of your flaws and quirks. The truth is that we are all imperfect humans, and it is precisely this that makes us unique and extraordinary.

Embracing your imperfections does not mean giving up on personal growth or settling for mediocrity. On the contrary, it is an act of authenticity and courage. When you embrace your flaws, you are freeing yourself from the shackles of constant self-criticism, thus creating space for healthy development. Remember, no one is perfect, and the pursuit of perfection only serves to undermine your self-esteem.

Accepting your individuality is also essential in building your self-esteem. Each of us is distinct, with our own unique talents, interests, and attributes. In a world that often promotes conformity, embracing what sets you apart is an empowering act. By allowing yourself to be authentic, you will attract people and situations that value you for who you are, not for who you try to be to please others. Here are some ways to practice accepting your imperfections and embracing your individuality:

Understanding Acceptance

Understanding acceptance is vital for nurturing lasting, healthy self-esteem. People often misunderstand acceptance, equating it with condoning negative behaviors or lacking the drive for personal growth. However, genuine acceptance is an act of courage and authenticity that allows you to approach yourself with compassion and love, regardless of your imperfections.

Accepting your imperfections does not mean ignoring areas of your life that need improvement. Quite the contrary, it involves recognizing that no one is perfect; we all make mistakes and have aspects that require continuous growth. Acceptance is about embracing the complete human being you are, with all your strengths and weaknesses.

Acceptance also does not mean settling for negative or harmful standards in your life. It is important to distinguish between acceptance and tolerating behaviors that do not serve you. Through unconditional self-acceptance, you gain the clarity and strength needed to make decisions that promote your well-being and growth. Here are some key points to understanding acceptance:

Unconditional Self-Love: Accepting yourself unconditionally is an act of self-love. It means recognizing your intrinsic worth as a human being, regardless of circumstances or external achievements.

Balancing Acceptance and Growth: Acceptance is not a hindrance to personal growth; it provides a strong foundation for growth by allowing you to learn from your mistakes and evolve from your experiences.

Authenticity and Vulnerability: Acceptance requires authenticity and vulnerability. It is a courageous choice to show up as your authentic self, without the need to mask your imperfections.

Self-Empowerment: Through self-acceptance, you take control of your narrative. You cast aside external expectations and embrace your true identity.

Distinguishing Change from Authenticity: Acceptance does not impede your pursuit of improvement in life. However, these changes should come from a place of authenticity and self-compassion, rather than from a need to conform to external standards.

Acknowledging Mistakes and Shortcomings: Acceptance involves acknowledging that we all make mistakes and face challenges. This allows you to release excessive self-criticism and become kinder to yourself.

Cultivating Self-Compassion: Acceptance is an extension of self-compassion. When you accept yourself, you choose to treat yourself with the same kindness and compassion you would offer to a dear friend.

Present-Moment Focus: Acceptance helps you live in the present moment. Instead of worrying about the past or the future, you focus on accepting and embracing the now.

Understanding the true nature of acceptance is an essential step in building a strong self-esteem. By embracing your imperfections and unconditionally accepting yourself, you create space for a healthier, more authentic relationship with yourself and others. Acceptance not only strengthens your self-esteem, but it also allows you to flourish as the unique and valuable individual you are.

Discerning Destructive Self-Critique

Before nurturing a healthy self-esteem and embracing your imperfections, it is essential to recognize and discern the patterns of destructive self-critique that may be undermining your confidence and emotional well-being. Destructive self-critique is that inner critical voice that questions your worth, judges your actions, and contributes to feelings of inadequacy.

Self-Awareness of Thought Patterns: The first step in identifying destructive self-critique is to cultivate self-awareness of your thought patterns. Pay attention to times when you find yourself thinking negatively about yourself. These thoughts often manifest automatically and subtly, becoming ingrained as habitual tendencies.

Reflective Inquiries: When caught in a cycle of self-critique, ask yourself the following questions to identify and challenge these thought patterns:

Are these thoughts realistic? Scrutinize whether your self-critical thoughts are rooted in reality or if they are exaggerated and distorted.

What are the origins of these beliefs? Try to discern the origins of the beliefs that fuel your self-critique. This can help you understand why you criticize yourself in such a way.

Are you being overly harsh on yourself? Evaluate whether you are imposing an unrealistic standard of perfection on yourself, not allowing for errors and imperfections.

How would you speak to a friend? Ask yourself how you would respond to a friend facing the same situation. Often, you will be more kind and understanding towards others than towards yourself.

What evidence contradicts these thoughts? Seek evidence in your life that contradicts your self-critical thoughts. This can help balance your perspective.

How can you support yourself? Instead of criticizing, consider how you can support and encourage yourself in the same way you would a friend.

Cultivating a Self-Compassion Mindset: Once you have identified destructive self-critique, you can begin to develop a self-compassion mindset. This involves replacing self-criticism with a more gentle and compassionate inner dialogue. Self-compassion acknowledges that we are all human beings who are susceptible to errors and imperfections, which does not diminish our worth.

Understand that the process of identifying and overcoming destructive self-critique is ongoing. As you become more conscious of your negative thought patterns, you can begin to challenge and replace them with a more positive and compassionate mindset. This will not only boost your self-esteem, but it will also foster a healthier and more loving internal environment.

Confronting Limiting Beliefs

Challenging limiting beliefs is a key step on the journey to building strong self-esteem and nurturing a healthier self-love. Limiting beliefs are deeply rooted negative thoughts that shape our perception of ourselves and the world around us. By acknowledging and confronting these beliefs, we can cultivate a more positive and constructive mindset. Here are some tips for confronting limiting beliefs:

Inquire Into the Genesis of Beliefs: A significant starting point is to question the origin of these limiting beliefs. Where do they come from? Are they based on past experiences, external expectations, or unfavorable comparisons with others? By pinpointing the sources of these beliefs, we can begin to understand why they exist.

Seek Counter-Evidence: An effective strategy involves seeking evidence that contradicts these limiting beliefs. Look for instances in your life where you've challenged or overcome these beliefs. This can help to dismantle the negative self-view and construct a fresh perspective rooted in affirmative facts.

Rewrite the Narrative: As you confront limiting beliefs, begin the process of rewriting your self-narrative. Replace negative beliefs with positive and realistic affirmations. For instance, if you've habitually believed yourself to be "incapable," rewrite this belief as "I am capable of learning and growing through effort and dedication."

Gain Outside Perspectives: Engaging in conversations with trusted friends, family, or a therapist can provide external perspectives on your limiting beliefs. Sometimes, those around us can see our potential more clearly than we can ourselves.

Embark on Gradual Transformation: The challenge of confronting limiting beliefs is not an overnight process, but rather an incremental transformation. Every instance of questioning and contesting a negative belief lays the foundation for a more constructive thought pattern. Remember, just as these beliefs were woven over time, they can also be unwoven over time.

Commend Progress: With each venture into challenging and reshaping limiting beliefs, celebrate every small triumph. Every instance of replacing a negative belief with a positive one fortifies our self-esteem and erects a sturdier bedrock for self-love.

In confronting limiting beliefs, we reshape the way we perceive and relate to ourselves. This process of self-transformation is essential to building a sound and nurturing self-esteem, granting us liberation from the shackles of the past and guiding us towards becoming more authentic and self-assured versions of ourselves.

Nurturing Self-Compassion

Self-compassion is a powerful tool for tending to your self-esteem and self-love. It involves treating yourself with kindness, respect, and compassion, regardless of mistakes or imperfections. The practice of self-compassion empowers you to create an inner sanctuary where you can confront challenges, learn from your setbacks, and grow as an individual.

Often, we are harsher on ourselves than we are on anyone else. Self-compassion is the art of extending the same compassion and kindness that you would offer to a dear friend. When you make a mistake, instead of harshly criticizing yourself, you comfort and embrace yourself. This does not mean avoiding responsibility; rather, it means providing yourself with an inner haven of support and acceptance. Self-compassion has three essential components:

Self-Kindness: Treating yourself with kindness and tenderness, especially in times of difficulty or mistakes.

Shared Humanity: Recognizing that being human is being imperfect, and we all face challenges and mistakes. This helps to mitigate the sense of isolation in your experiences.

Mindfulness: Being aware of your present feelings without judgment. This allows you to acknowledge your emotions and thoughts without excessively identifying with them.

Benefits of Self-Compassion: Nurturing self-compassion has many benefits for your mental and emotional well-being, including:

Stress Reduction: Self-compassion reduces stress levels by preventing unnecessary self-imposed pressure and reducing excessive self-criticism.

Resilience: When you treat yourself with compassion, you are cultivating emotional resilience to face life's challenges.

Fortified Self-Esteem: Self-compassion helps to build healthier self-esteem, as you recognize your inherent worth regardless of mistakes.

Self-Acceptance: The practice of self-compassion gives you permission to embrace yourself with all your flaws and blemishes, fostering a sense of authenticity.

Enhanced Relationships: By cultivating self-compassion, you learn to treat yourself with greater tenderness, which can reverberate in your interactions with others.

Celebrate Your Distinctions

Celebrating your distinctions is an integral part of the journey toward self-love and self-esteem. In a world that often emphasizes conformity and normative patterns, acknowledging and cherishing what makes you unique is an act of authenticity and empowerment.

The Beauty of Diversity: Imagine a world where everyone is exactly the same. There would be no creativity, no diversity of perspectives, and no innovation. Diversity is what makes the world interesting, exciting, and vibrant. Each individual brings a unique story, unique experiences, and unique qualities that enrich the tapestry of humanity.

Transforming Quirks into Strengths: The quirks you possess are opportunities for expressing your authentic self. Instead of viewing them as negatives, consider them as facets that make you unique and valuable. The ability to transform your quirks into strengths is a testament to your self-confidence and self-love.

Self-Expression and Authenticity: Celebrating your differences has a powerful impact on self-expression. When you feel comfortable being yourself without fear of judgment, you are deeply connected to your true identity. This empowers you to navigate life with confidence, rather than trying to fit into preconceived molds.

Challenging Standardized Thinking: Standardized thinking involves comparing your attributes and accomplishments against a fixed standard. This can lead to self-criticism and feelings of inadequacy. However, by celebrating your differences, you challenge this standardized thinking and open the door to a more positive mindset.

Embracing the Journey of Self-Discovery: Celebrating your distinctions is closely intertwined with the ongoing journey of self-discovery. As you delve into who you are, you uncover your preferences, passions, and individual values. This exploration helps you forge a deeper connection with yourself and create a more comprehensive and accurate self-image.

Commending Small Triumphs: Remember that every time you embrace a quirk or act in accordance with your convictions, you are celebrating a small victory. These moments of self-assertion contribute to the gradual construction of your self-esteem and self-love.

Embracing Initial Discomfort: It's important to note that while celebrating your differences can be empowering, it can also initially feel uncomfortable. This is due to exposure to societal expectations and the fear of judgment. However, with time and practice, this discomfort tends to fade, and you become more confident in your uniqueness.

Inspiration for Others: When you celebrate your distinctions, you become a source of inspiration for those around you. Your authenticity encourages others to also embrace who they are and to express themselves freely.

By celebrating your differences, you are laying a solid foundation for your self-esteem and self-love. You are choosing to live life on your own terms, embracing the inner diversity that makes you exceptional. This celebration not only strengthens your relationship with yourself, but it also contributes to the creation of a more inclusive and accepting world.

Cultivating a Growth Mindset

A growth mindset is a powerful tool that can transform your journey toward self-love and the cultivation of healthy relationships. This mindset is based on the belief that your abilities, intelligence, and personality can grow and develop over time through effort, learning, and resilience.

Errors as Learning Opportunities: One of the cornerstones of a growth mindset is the ability to see errors and setbacks as learning opportunities. Instead of feeling discouraged when you make mistakes, you embrace them as opportunities to gain valuable insights and lessons that can be applied in the future.

Redefining Failure: Within the framework of a growth mindset, failure is not the end of the road, but rather a starting point. It is an opportunity to identify areas that need improvement, to experiment with different approaches, and ultimately to achieve success through trial and error.

Value in All Experiences: When you adopt a growth mindset, you begin to see value in all experiences, whether positive or challenging. Every experience contributes to your growth by providing you with insights into your skills, preferences, and areas that need development.

Resilience and Persistence: A growth mindset is inherently linked to resilience and persistence. You recognize that success does not come overnight, but requires ongoing effort. Adversities are seen as opportunities to strengthen your resilience and increase your capacity to overcome obstacles.

Learning from Critiques and Feedback: In a growth mindset, you embrace critiques and feedback as valuable input for your development. Instead of feeling discouraged by criticism, you view these external perspectives as a means to enhance and refine your skills.

Persevering in the Face of Challenges: When faced with challenges, a growth mindset encourages you to persevere. Instead of giving up, you focus on learning from the challenge and devising ways to overcome it.

Fostering Confidence: A growth mindset contributes to the development of self-confidence. As you recognize your progress and accomplishments over time, your self-assurance naturally grows.

Developing a growth mindset is an ongoing investment in yourself. This approach not only strengthens your self-esteem, but also empowers you to face life with resilience, optimism, and a constructive outlook on all aspects of your journey.

Shift Your Focus

Redirecting your focus is a powerful strategy to boost your self-love and cultivate healthy relationships. Often, we tend to fixate our gaze solely on the areas we deem negative, inadvertently underestimating our own qualities and achievements. By directing your attention towards your positive attributes and accomplishments, you are sculpting a more balanced and uplifting perspective of yourself.

Balancing Self-Assessment: Self-assessment is important, but it must be balanced. Rather than exclusively fixating on your weaknesses, mistakes, or areas you wish to change, set aside time to acknowledge your positive qualities and successes. This will help you create a more comprehensive and realistic self-image.

Uncovering Your Positive Qualities: We often undervalue our own positive qualities. Take some time to identify and recognize these attributes. Ask your friends, family, and colleagues what they perceive as positive in you. Sometimes, gaining external perspectives can illuminate facets you may not have noticed.

Celebrating Your Achievements: Our achievements deserve to be celebrated, no matter how seemingly trivial. Each step towards a goal, every personal triumph, and each challenge overcome represents a milestone on your journey. Take a moment to acknowledge these triumphs and revel in your progress.

Cultivating a Positive Self-Image: By shifting your focus to your positive attributes, you are contributing to the cultivation of a positive self-image. You begin to see yourself as someone of value, potential, and the ability to positively impact both your life and the lives of others.

Challenging Positive Self-Reflection: Challenge yourself to engage in regular positive self-reflection. Think about three things you did well or are proud of during the day. This will help you counterbalance the tendency to fixate on what went wrong.

Deconstructing Negative Bias: Negative bias is the inclination to assign greater weight to negative experiences than positive ones. Become aware of this bias and actively challenge it. When you catch yourself fixating on the negative, redirect your attention to the positive.

List of Achievements: Create a catalog of your achievements over time. Include major accomplishments as well as minor daily successes. This list will serve as a tangible reminder of your capacity to achieve and progress.

Practicing Gratitude: Gratitude practice also contributes to shifting focus towards the positive. Regularly reflect on things you are grateful for, whether they pertain to your qualities, achievements, or daily experiences.

Visualizing a Positive Self: Use visualization to imagine yourself as a confident, accomplished, and capable individual. This technique can help to fortify a positive self-image.

By shifting your focus towards your positive qualities and accomplishments, you are building a strong foundation for lasting positive self-esteem and self-love. This practice not only shapes your own perspective, but it also influences how you interact with others, fostering a more positive and uplifting atmosphere in all facets of your life.

Embrace Authenticity

The practice of authenticity embarks on a journey of self-discovery and empowerment that fortifies your self-esteem and self-love. To be authentic is to be true to oneself in all facets of life, regardless of external expectations or societal pressures. This approach helps to forge more genuine relationships and nurture a profound sense of self-confidence.

The Essence of Authenticity: To be authentic means to integrate your beliefs, values, and personality into your actions and expressions. Rather than concealing who you are, you allow yourself to radiate with your true essence. Authenticity is a declaration of self-love, where you put yourself first and recognize that you deserve to be loved and accepted exactly as you are.

Genuine Connection with Others: When you are authentic, you foster true and deep connections with others. By revealing your true self, you allow those around you to know and accept you for who you are. This fosters an environment of mutual trust and respect.

Overcoming the Fear of Judgment: One of the greatest hurdles to authenticity is the fear of others' judgment.

However, by practicing authenticity, you are choosing your own internal validation over seeking external approval. This helps to relinquish the need to fit into predefined molds and find freedom in expressing your true identity.

Celebrating Individuality: Authenticity celebrates individuality and acknowledges that everyone has something unique to offer. When you allow yourself to be authentic, you are celebrating your uniqueness and sharing your distinctive qualities with the world.

Practicing authenticity is a choice that demands courage and commitment, yet the benefits are immeasurable. By allowing yourself to be authentic, you are creating space for a life of fulfillment, satisfaction, and meaningful relationships, all rooted in the acceptance of your core self.

Eradicate Self-Labeling

Eradicating self-labeling is an essential practice for fostering self-love and cultivating healthy relationships. Labeling yourself with negative adjectives constrains your self-perception and limits your growth potential. By relinquishing these self-labels, you create space for a path of continuous self-discovery and self-acceptance.

The Hazards of Negative Labels: When you label yourself with negative adjectives, you are creating a limited and distorted self-image. These labels can impact your self-esteem and shape your perception of your own capabilities. Furthermore, negative labels can become self-fulfilling prophecies, where you act in accordance with these self-imposed expectations.

The Truth of Personal Evolution: Recognizing oneself as an ever-evolving individual is an integral part of self-love cultivation. Change is a constant in life and each experience, mistake and learning contributes to your growth. Instead of clinging to fixed labels, allow yourself to change and develop over time.

Rewriting the Inner Dialogue: Self-labeling often manifests as negative self-talk. Identify these thoughts and begin to rewrite this dialogue. Rather than saying "I am a failure," shift it to "I am learning from my challenges and growing from them."

The Challenge of Self-Reflection: Challenge yourself to regularly reflect on how you internally label yourself. Ask whether these labels are truly accurate or merely distorted perceptions based on specific moments.

Embracing Complexity: Each person is a complex blend of qualities, experiences, and emotions. By eliminating self-labeling, you are embracing this complexity and acknowledging that your identity cannot be reduced to a single adjective.

Treating Yourself with Compassion: When you catch yourself labeling yourself negatively, practice self-compassion. Treat yourself with the same kindness you would extend to a dear friend. Understand that everyone faces moments of challenge, but those moments do not define your entirety.

Recognizing Your Achievements: By focusing on your evolution, you acknowledge your past achievements. Every step you've taken toward growth stands as a testament to your ability to overcome challenges.

Affirming Your Potential: Substitute negative self-labels with affirmations of your potential and capabilities. Realize that you possess the power to grow, learn, and change.

Embracing the Fluidity of Identity: Identity is not static; it's fluid and constantly changing. By eradicating self-labeling, you're making room to embrace this fluidity and to be amazed by the various versions of yourself throughout life.

Eliminating self-labeling is a journey of self-discovery and growth. By freeing yourself from negative labels, you're choosing to see yourself as an ever-evolving being, poised to embrace new experiences, learn from challenges, and build a solid and empowered self-love.

Seek Inspiration from Authentic Role Models

Seeking inspiration from authentic role models is a powerful way to strengthen your journey of self-love and the cultivation of healthy relationships. Observing and connecting with individuals who embody authenticity and embrace their own imperfections can offer valuable insights and inspire you to walk the path of genuineness.

Learning from Positive Examples: By seeking inspiration from authentic role models, you expose yourself to positive examples of how to live an authentic and genuine life. Witnessing how these individuals handle their own imperfections and express themselves truthfully can be a fountain of valuable learning.

Valuing Authenticity: Authentic role models showcase that authenticity is precious and worthy of celebration. Observing how they are embraced and respected for their authenticity helps you understand the value of being true to yourself.

Challenging Social Norms: The pursuit of authentic role models can challenge societal standards of appearance, behavior, and success. These models demonstrate that you need not fit into predefined molds to be loved and cherished.

Forging Meaningful Relationships: By drawing inspiration from authentic role models, you might be motivated to seek relationships founded on truth and mutual acceptance. This can lead to deeper and more authentic connections with individuals who share similar values.

The Journey of Self-Discovery: Understand that, as you seek inspiration from authentic role models, you are on your own journey of self-discovery. Every person is unique, and their experiences and challenges differ. Use these models as a source of guidance, but also trust your intuition and what resonates with your inner truth.

Seeking inspiration from authentic role models is a way to nurture your experience of self-discovery, self-love, and the cultivation of meaningful relationships. By observing how others embrace their authenticity, you become more empowered to live a life aligned with your true essence and values.

PRACTICAL EXERCISES
TO CULTIVATE SELF-ESTEEM

In addition to embracing your imperfections, there are practical exercises that can help you cultivate and strengthen your self-esteem. These exercises are designed to help you shift your perspective in a positive way and engage with the world around you with more confidence.

Letter of Self-Love: Write a letter to yourself as if you were addressing a dear friend. List your qualities, accomplishments, and attributes that you admire in yourself. Read this letter whenever you need a positive reminder.

Compassion Journal: Keep a journal where you write down messages of self-compassion whenever you catch yourself criticizing yourself. Write kind and encouraging words to yourself, just as you would for a friend going through a difficult time.

Visual Acceptance Practice: Look into a mirror and lock eyes with your own reflection. Instead of focusing on your imperfections, focus on the features that you cherish about yourself. Say aloud or to yourself: "I accept and love myself as I am."

List of Personal Triumphs: Make a list of all your personal triumphs, big or small. This could include things like learning a new skill, overcoming a challenge, or simply maintaining a positive attitude during difficult times. Use this list to remind yourself of your accomplishments whenever you feel self-doubt.

Authenticity Visualization: Engage in creative visualization by imagining yourself living authentically and wholeheartedly embracing your true self. Visualize scenarios where you feel confident, fulfilled, and connected to yourself.

Personal Care Ritual: Create a personal care ritual that is meaningful to you. This may include taking a relaxing bath, walking in nature, meditating, or practicing yoga. Dedicate time regularly to take care of yourself and replenish your energy.

Positive Affirmations: Create positive affirmations that reinforce your self-esteem and self-acceptance. Repeat these affirmations daily, preferably in the morning, to set a positive mindset for the day.

It is important to remember that building self-esteem is a continuous and gradual process. Do not expect overnight results, but be willing to invest time and effort in nurturing a healthy and loving relationship with yourself. As you embrace acceptance and self-care, you will strengthen your self-esteem and lay a solid foundation for healthy relationships and a more fulfilling life.

CHAPTER 4

FORGING A BOND WITHIN

In the grand ballet of life,
discover your soul
as the perfect partner.

The construction of healthy relationships and self-love remains an elusive feat until you unveil a profound understanding of your essence. The connection with oneself serves as the cornerstone upholding all other connections in your existence. In this chapter, we shall delve into the odyssey of self-awareness, embarking on practices and methods of integration into your life's tapestry.

THE ODYSSEY TOWARDS SELF-DISCOVERY

The odyssey towards self-discovery is an ongoing and captivating exploration of your very being. It beckons you to delve deep into the recesses of your mind, heart, and experiences, all to fathom your motivations, beliefs, and desires. This journey is an act of self-love, for the more you acquaint yourself, the more empowered you become in making choices that resonate with your true essence.

Unveiling Your Personal Saga

Your personal saga is a trove of experiences, moments, and challenges that have forged the person you are today. When you embark upon your saga, you plunge into the profound layers of your identity and unearth the threads that have woven the unique tapestry of your life. Exploring your personal saga stands as a profound way to connect with yourself and construct a richer understanding of your lived experience.

Reflecting on Childhood: Childhood is a realm of discovery, exploration, and formation of foundational beliefs. Reflect upon the memories of your early years. What were your interests? Which activities ignited your enthusiasm? What were your dreams? These memories may unveil clues about your enduring passions and motivations.

Delving into Defining Experiences: Defining experiences can span from jubilant occasions to formidable challenges. Ponder upon moments that have left a deep imprint on your being. How have these experiences influenced your perspectives and choices? What lessons have they imparted? By delving into these experiences, you might unearth a greater understanding of your resilience and capacity for growth.

Triumphs Overcome: The challenges you've surmounted stand as testimonials to your inner strength. Contemplate how you faced adversities in your life. What skills did you cultivate to surmount these hurdles? How have these challenges molded your outlook and fostered your growth? These experiences might reveal essential facets of your resilience and determination.

Pinnacles of Achievement: Celebrate your moments of achievement and triumph. They are evidences of your abilities, endeavors, and aspirations. Reflect upon what you've accomplished and how it made you feel. These moments not only signify your accomplishments but can also shed light on your passions and areas where you shine.

Connecting the Dots: As you explore your personal saga, begin connecting the dots between your experiences. Seek out patterns, recurring themes, and transformative moments. You might discover that certain events or themes play a pivotal role in shaping your identity and life's direction.

Penning Your Narrative: Consider penning your own personal narrative. This need not be a formal endeavor; you can simply begin recording your memories, experiences, and reflections. As your narrative unfolds, you may gain a deeper understanding of your motivations, values, and ambitions.

An Ongoing Journey of Discovery: Exploring your personal saga is an ongoing journey. As you evolve, your perspective may shift, revealing new layers of understanding. Embrace this journey as an opportunity to know yourself more profoundly, as you lay a firm foundation for authenticity, self-love, and the cultivation of healthy relationships.

Discovering Your Core Values

Your core values are the cornerstones of your individuality. They reflect the principles you hold essential for guiding your decisions, actions, and life's course. By identifying and understanding your values, you acquire an internal compass that steers you towards a more authentic and fulfilling life.

Embarking on Value Exploration: Uncovering your core values demands an inward journey of exploration. Ask yourself questions about the qualities you hold most paramount in yourself and others. What principles are non-negotiable? Consider a spectrum of life domains: ethics, relationships, career, spirituality, and societal contribution.

Discerning Significant Values: As you venture forth, you're likely to amass a list of values that resonate with you. Refine this list to those that truly strike a chord in your heart and harmonize with your inner truth. Remember, your values are personal and unique to you—there are no right or wrong answers.

Hierarchy of Values: Once you've identified your values, ranking them by importance can be helpful. This helps you understand which values take precedence in your decisions and which might play a secondary role. For example, freedom might outweigh financial security in importance.

Aligned Decision-Making: Your values serve as a compass in decision-making. When you're mindful of your core values, you can evaluate available options based on how well they align with what you deem paramount. This leads to choices that resonate with your true essence and life's direction.

The Journey of Authenticity: Unearthing your core values is a pivotal part of the journey towards authenticity. Living in accordance with your values ushers in a profound sense of congruence and contentment. They provide a yardstick against which to measure your choices and actions, empowering you to craft a life that is genuinely your own.

Values' Evolution: It's important to recognize that your values can evolve over time. As you grow and mature, your priorities might shift. Be willing to revisit and reevaluate your values as life guides you down new pathways.

A Trustworthy Inner Compass: Your core values serve as an internal compass that steers your choices and actions. Embracing your authentic values is tantamount to building a solid foundation for a life grounded in authenticity, self-love, and alignment with what holds profound significance for you.

The Significance of Passions and Interests

Uncovering and nurturing your passions and interests is like igniting an inner light that illuminates the path of self-discovery. These are the realms where you forge the deepest connection with yourself, where time seems to dissolve, and you find a constant wellspring of joy and motivation. Identifying and nurturing your passions is a pivotal part of constructing an authentic and meaningful life.

Embarking on the Energetic Quest: To unearth your passions, ponder over activities that make you feel most alive and engaged. Ask yourself: What do I love doing? What brings a genuine smile to my face? Which subjects or hobbies captivate and sustain my interest? As you immerse yourself in these pursuits, take heed of the sensations of enthusiasm and vitality they evoke.

The Depths of Connection: Authentic passions and interests are those that allow for a profound connection with your essence. You become engrossed and submerged in the activity, losing track of time and concern. This profound connection signals that you are touching on authentic facets of who you are.

Sources of Authenticity: Your passions and interests unveil authentic facets of your personality. When you engage in activities you love, you honor your true essence. This fosters a sense of congruence between your actions and values, forming a sturdy foundation for self-love and authenticity.

Guiding Your Life: Passions and interests not only bring immediate joy but can also powerfully steer your life. When you acknowledge and pursue your passions, you align with your authentic direction. This can lead to more fulfilling career choices, more significant connections, and a deeper sense of purpose.

Crafting a Meaningful Existence: Passions and interests are like the ingredients that flavor your life. As you cultivate these authentic aspects of yourself, you are constructing a life that is rich in meaning and contentment. Your passions not only connect you with yourself but also enrich your relationship with the world around you.

A Beacon for the Path: Your passions serve as a beacon that lights the path to authenticity and lasting happiness. By following what you love, you choose a path of congruence and authenticity. Allowing your passions to guide your journey, you are crafting a life that is undeniably yours, shaped by your authentic ardor and joy.

Exploring the Vistas of Life Goals

Your life goals are like the stars that guide your journey. They not only represent tangible milestones you strive to attain but also reflect your deepest desires, dreams, and aspirations. In the exploration and delineation of your goals, you chart the course for a life aligned with your values and passions, crafting a map for personal fulfillment and enduring happiness.

Contemplating Your Aspirations: Begin by reflecting on key domains of your life. Ask yourself: What do I desire to achieve in my career? What kind of relationships do I wish to nurture? How do I envision my personal growth? What impact do I seek to make on the world around me? In probing these realms, you commence identifying goals that hold genuine significance for you.

Goals Aligned with Values: Your life goals should resonate with your core values. They serve as tangible expressions of your inner principles. By defining goals that mirror your values, you ensure that your actions and achievements are congruent with your authentic self.

From Vision to Action: While life goals might encompass tangible milestones, such as professional accomplishments or financial targets, they can also pertain to personal growth, healthy relationships, and emotional well-being. Once you identify your aspirations, it's time to break them down into smaller, actionable steps. This metamorphoses your lofty visions into practical actions.

Guiding Your Choices: Your life goals stand as reliable beacons for your daily choices. They aid in prioritizing tasks, making decisions, and directing your focus. When presented with choices, inquire how each option draws you closer or farther from your life goals. This aids in making decisions that are more aligned and authentic.

Adapting to Evolution: Keep in mind that your life goals can evolve as you grow and transform. What holds importance today may shift over time. Be open to reassessing and adjusting your goals so they continually reflect your personal journey.

Erecting the Desired Life: Your life goals are like the building blocks composing the structure of the life you wish to construct. They are a steadfast reminder of what holds importance to you and what you aspire to achieve. By heeding your aspirations, you are constructing an authentic and meaningful life, sculpted by your passion, purpose, and core values.

The Role of Self-Reflection

Self-reflection is like a mirror that illuminates the internal landscapes of your mind and heart. It is a powerful tool for self-awareness, enabling you to delve deeply into your emotions, thoughts, and experiences. By dedicating regular time to engage in self-reflection, you create a space to connect with your inner journey, learn about yourself, and evolve meaningfully.

An Arena of Exploration: Self-reflection provides a safe arena to explore who you are, what you feel, and what you think. It offers an opportunity to unwind, detach from external distractions, and delve into the depths of your being. Within this space, new insights can be unearthed, behavioral patterns understood, and motivations clarified.

Reserving Time for Practice: Much like any skill, self-reflection demands consistent practice. Allocate moments daily or weekly to detach from the external world and attune to your inner experience. This can be accomplished through meditation, journaling, tranquil strolls, or simply sitting in silence.

Profound Inquiry: During self-reflection, pose probing questions that invite honest exploration. Query your present emotions, reactions to recent events, and the lessons you are learning. Ponder upon sources of joy, challenges faced, and your responses to them.

Emerging Patterns: Over time, you may discern behavioral, emotional, or mental patterns arising from your self-reflections. This can unveil trends that may have eluded your notice previously. For instance, you might realize you consistently take on extra responsibilities at work due to a deep-seated fear of disappointing others.

Cultivating Mindfulness: Self-reflection is a means to cultivate mindfulness, which is present-moment awareness of your internal experiences without judgment. By observing your emotions and thoughts with curiosity and acceptance, you create a space to fathom yourself at a deeper level.

Journaling: Maintaining a journal is an effective means to practice self-reflection. Chronicle your feelings, thoughts, experiences, and insights. Over time, perusing your entries reveals changes, progress, and areas that may warrant further attention.

Fostering Self-Connection: Self-reflection is an act of self-love and self-connection. By committing to this practice, you invest time and energy to understand, grow, and evolve. It aids in keeping you aligned with your inner journey, reminding you that authenticity and self-discovery are foundational to a meaningful life.

A Dialogue with Oneself: Self-reflection constitutes a silent dialogue you uphold with yourself. It's an opportunity to be your own friend, advisor, and impartial observer. Nurturing this relationship with yourself establishes a firm foundation for healthy self-esteem and a profound comprehension of your needs and desires.

EXERCISES TO CULTIVATE SELF-KNOWLEDGE

Cultivating self-knowledge is an ongoing commitment to oneself, an inner exploration that will lead to a profound understanding of one's own being. The following practices are potent tools to facilitate this process and forge a stronger connection with oneself:

Meditation and Contemplation

Meditation serves as a precious tool for delving into oneself on a deeper level. Regularly set aside time to meditate, granting yourself a serene space to observe your thoughts, emotions, and sensations. Reflection is equally pivotal; after meditating, allocate time to analyze and process what surfaced during the meditation.

Personal Journaling

Maintaining a journal is a powerful means of documenting your path to self-discovery. Write about your revelations, reflections, challenges, and achievements. A journal provides a safe haven to express your most intimate thoughts and helps track your progress over time.

Profound Questioning

Pose questions that transcend the surface. Inquire into your beliefs, motivations, and desires. Ask yourself about your greatest accomplishments, deepest fears, and what makes you feel truly alive. As you delve deeper into these inquiries, a clearer vision of who you are and what you yearn for emerges.

External Feedback

While self-knowledge is an internal journey, external feedback can also be enlightening. Ask close friends, family, or mentors how they perceive you. They may shed light on qualities, talents, and traits that you may not see in yourself.

Experimentation

Embark on new ventures as a way to uncover undiscovered facets of your personality. Venture into uncharted territory by trying new hobbies, activities, or experiences that you never thought of attempting. Not only does this expand your horizons, but it also allows you to discover hidden passions and aspects of yourself that may have been underestimated.

Continuous Journey of Self-Knowledge

It's important to recognize that self-knowledge is an ongoing journey, and these practices should be woven into your life on a regular basis. As you grow and evolve, your responses to meditations, reflections, and inquiries may also change. This signifies constant growth and learning.

The Path of Personal Development

The journey of self-discovery is as unique as the individual themselves. The outlined practices serve as guiding lights to help you delve into your identity, but it's essential to tailor them to your preferences and needs. As you deepen your relationship with yourself, you become more resilient, self-assured, and empowered to make decisions that are aligned with your true essence.

Time and Patience

Self-discovery is a process that takes time and patience. Be kind to yourself as you immerse yourself in these practices. There's no rush; the journey itself is precious and rewarding. The more you commit to nurturing self-awareness, the more you build a solid foundation for authenticity, self-love, and healthy relationships in your life.

INTEGRATING SELF-KNOWLEDGE INTO YOUR LIFE

The true value of self-knowledge lies in how you apply what you've learned to your daily existence. Infusing self-awareness into your everyday journey transforms inner insights into tangible external actions, leading to a more authentic and fulfilling life.

Making Aligned Decisions

Self-knowledge acts as an internal compass that guides your decision-making. When you understand your values, goals, and passions, you can make choices that are in harmony with your true essence. This prevents impulsive decisions and puts you in control of your life.

Cultivating Healthy Relationships

Understanding your own needs and boundaries is essential for nurturing healthy relationships. You can communicate your expectations and establish boundaries clearly and respectfully. Relationships grounded in self-awareness are more genuine, as both parties engage as their authentic selves, rather than trying to fit predefined roles.

Seeking Purpose

Self-knowledge is a powerful tool for setting goals and seeking a sense of purpose. By understanding your values and passions, you can steer your life towards meaningful objectives. Self-awareness also helps identify areas where you can uniquely contribute to the world, providing a profound sense of purpose.

Personalized Self-Care

Understanding your emotional, physical, and mental needs enables you to craft a personalized and effective self-care routine. You can identify self-care practices that genuinely rejuvenate you and step away from those that merely fill the void. This fosters a deeper and more sustainable sense of well-being.

Continual Growth

Self-discovery is a journey that never ends. Stay open to learning more about yourself throughout life. As you face new challenges and experiences, you will continue to learn, grow, and evolve. Maintaining a growth mindset is essential for ongoing development.

The journey toward self-awareness is a profound and rewarding quest to understand your essence. By uncovering your values, passions, and life goals, you pave the way for a more authentic connection with yourself, allowing self-love and relationships to flourish with authenticity and significance.

CHAPTER 5

EMBRACING THE RELEASE OF EMOTIONAL BURDENS

Unshackle the ties of the past
and soar towards a lighter heart.

Throughout the journey of life, we accumulate emotional experiences that shape our perception of ourselves and the world around us. Some of these experiences can be positive and enriching, while others might be past traumas, negative patterns, and unprocessed emotions that metamorphose into emotional baggage. In this chapter, we will delve into strategies and approaches to address these burdens, unburdening the weight they exert upon our relationships, emotional well-being, and personal development.

CONFRONTING PAST TRAUMAS AND NEGATIVE PATTERNS

The path to self-love is not solely about embracing the beautiful facets of ourselves, but also about confronting the emotional wounds that may be holding us back. Past traumas and negative patterns can give rise to emotional baggage that affects our self-esteem, relationships, and overall well-being. Within this chapter, we will explore strategies to handle these burdens, transmuting them into opportunities for healing and growth.

Recognizing Emotional Wounds

Before embarking on the journey of emotional healing, it is essential to closely examine the wounds we carry. These wounds may have deep roots and can result from a range of experiences, from traumatic events to negative patterns in relationships. Acknowledging these emotional wounds is the first step towards healing, as it allows us to bring to the surface what has often been kept hidden or suppressed.

Childhood Traumas and Past Experiences: Childhood traumas, such as neglect, emotional or physical abuse, can have a lasting impact on our adult lives. The wounds left by these experiences may manifest as insecurity, low self-esteem, and difficulties with trust. Identifying how these experiences have shaped our beliefs and behaviors is crucial for healing.

Toxic Relationships and Rejection: Toxic relationships or experiences of rejection can leave deep marks on our heart and mind. These wounds can manifest as a fear of emotional vulnerability, difficulty in trusting others, and a persistent sense of inadequacy. Recognizing how these experiences have affected us is an important step in breaking negative patterns.

Self-Criticism and Self-Sabotage Patterns: Often, we carry internalized emotional wounds, manifested by patterns of self-criticism and self-sabotage. These wounds may have roots in negative messages we received throughout our lives, resulting in a negative self-image and a lack of confidence in our abilities. Identifying these self-destructive patterns is pivotal for our emotional healing.

Acceptance and Compassion: Acknowledging our emotional wounds requires a deep level of self-acceptance and compassion. We often tend to judge or blame ourselves for our wounds, perpetuating the cycle of suffering. By allowing ourselves to feel and recognize these wounds without judgment, we create a safe space for healing.

Exploring the Origin of Wounds: While recognizing our emotional wounds, it is also important to explore their origins. This involves looking back into our life history and identifying the moments or patterns that contributed to the emergence of these wounds. Understanding how these wounds developed helps us better comprehend their influence on our current emotions and behaviors.

Effects on Relationships and Self-Care: Our emotional wounds not only impact our relationship with ourselves, but can also influence our relationships and our capacity for self-care. Untreated wounds can create communication barriers, promote destructive interaction patterns, and hinder our ability to establish deep and healthy connections.

Embracing the Pain

Confronting emotional wounds can be a painful journey, but it is a pivotal step toward healing. Instead of avoiding or suppressing these uncomfortable emotions, it is important to consciously embrace the pain in order to release and transform it.

Accepting Discomforting Emotions: The first step in embracing pain is to acknowledge the discomforting emotions that arise. We often tend to shy away from pain, whether by immersing ourselves in activities, negating our feelings, or avoiding the confrontation of our authentic emotions. However, in negating our pain, we also negate the opportunity to heal and grow.

Allowing Yourself to Feel: Embracing pain means allowing yourself to experience emotions fully and without judgment. This means making room for tears, sadness, anger, or any other emotion that may surface. Rather than stifling or veiling these feelings, allow yourself to fully experience them, recognizing that they are an integral part of the human experience.

Exercising Self-Awareness: Self-awareness plays a pivotal role in the process of embracing pain. By tuning into your emotions, you can discern when you are avoiding or suppressing uncomfortable feelings. The practice of self-awareness involves observing your emotional and physical responses in the face of challenging situations, enabling you to identify and embrace the pain that may be present.

Healthy Expression of Emotions: Uncovering healthy avenues for expressing your emotions is paramount during the process of embracing pain. Journaling, creating art, engaging in physical activity, or confiding in a trusted individual are ways to unburden repressed emotions. These endeavors not only allow you to connect with your emotions, but they also aid in transforming emotional energy into constructive output.

Embracing Yourself with Kindness: Embracing pain is an act of self-love. By permitting yourself to feel and express your emotions, you demonstrate that you deserve to be treated with kindness and compassion, especially in difficult moments. Self-compassion plays a pivotal role here, reminding you that your emotions are valid and that you deserve support and care throughout the entire healing process.

Transformation Through Unshackling: Embracing pain is a powerful step in the journey of emotional healing. By allowing emotions to flow organically, you are releasing accumulated energy and creating room for transformation. Be aware that pain does not define who you are; it is a transient facet of your journey toward self-discovery and growth. In embracing pain with love and acceptance, you are cultivating fertile soil to flourish into a sturdier and more authentic version of yourself.

Reconstructing Adverse Patterns

The redefinition of negative patterns is a pivotal step in the journey of emotional healing. Frequently, these patterns develop as defense mechanisms following painful experiences; however, they can metamorphose into impediments to growth and emotional well-being. Here, we will explore the art of identifying, interrogating, and reconstructing these negative patterns.

The Roots of Negative Patterns: Negative patterns may arise as forms of self-preservation after traumatic or painful experiences. They might manifest as ceaseless self-criticism, the fear of abandonment, challenges in setting boundaries, or the inclination to engage in toxic relationships. Recognizing these patterns serves as the first step in dismantling their sway over your life.

Challenging the Validity of Patterns: Once the negative patterns are acknowledged, it becomes imperative to question their validity. Frequently, these patterns are founded on limiting beliefs that have germinated from past experiences. Ask yourself if these patterns still hold relevance or if they are vestiges of events no longer enmeshed within your present life.

Identifying Destructive Patterns: Scrutinizing your recurrent emotional responses and behaviors can aid in identifying destructive patterns. Inquire into the triggers of these automatic reactions and how they impact your life. By identifying these patterns, you empower yourself to interrupt them and make more mindful decisions.

Substituting Patterns with Fresh Narratives: After challenging the validity of negative patterns, it is time to supplant them with novel narratives. This entails nurturing thoughts and beliefs that are healthier and more realistic. For instance, if you habitually subject yourself to excessive self-critique, replace it with self-compassion, acknowledging your worthiness of kindness and support.

Exercising Behavioral Shift: Altering negative patterns involves not only shifting thoughts, but also modifying behaviors. For instance, if you are accustomed to engaging in toxic relationships, endeavor to establish robust boundaries and opt for relationships grounded in mutual respect and support. Action constitutes an essential step in pattern redefinition.

The Sanctuary of Self-Compassion: Redefining negative patterns requires self-compassion. As you strive to make changes, remember that it is human to err and that the journey of transforming old patterns can be difficult. Be gentle with yourself and acknowledge that each step towards change is a step in the right direction.

Empowering Toward a Fresh Reality: Redefining negative patterns is an act of profound empowerment. It gives you authority over your life, allowing you to change patterns that no longer serve your growth and well-being. By questioning, replacing, and altering these patterns, you are creating space for a new reality based on self-esteem, healthy relationships, and authenticity.

Seeking Professional Support

Acknowledging the need for professional help in navigating emotional wounds is an act of self-empowerment. A skilled therapist can provide invaluable guidance and a safe environment to explore your deepest emotions, offering tailored tools and strategies to aid in healing. Let's delve into why seeking professional support is important and how it can positively impact your self-healing journey.

The Profundity of Emotional Wounds: Some traumas and emotional wounds can be so intricate and profound that they require a more specialized approach to healing.

When the pain feels overwhelmingly daunting to face alone, a trained therapist can provide the necessary expertise to guide you through the healing process in a healthy and effective way.

The Therapist's Role: A therapist is an individual trained to understand the intricacies of human emotions and the various therapeutic approaches available to address emotional wounds. They can create a safe, non-judgmental space where you can explore your emotions, decipher negative thought patterns, and develop coping strategies.

Tailored Treatment: Each individual is unique, and their emotional wounds are equally distinct. A therapist can customize the treatment according to your specific needs. They will help identify which therapeutic techniques are most appropriate for you, whether it is cognitive-behavioral therapy, exposure therapy, acceptance and commitment therapy, or other approaches.

Constructing Coping Tools: A therapist can teach you techniques and coping tools that you can integrate into your daily life to navigate challenging moments. This includes strategies for managing anxiety, regulating intense emotions, and restructuring negative thought patterns. These tools are invaluable resources that can help you address emotional challenges in a healthier way.

Profound Exploration and Self-Discovery: Therapeutic support can facilitate a deeper exploration of your emotional wounds and the narratives that surround them. They can help uncover connections between past experiences and present behavioral patterns, promoting richer self-discovery and a comprehensive understanding of how your emotions intertwine.

Transformation and Growth: The pursuit of professional support is not just about healing emotional wounds; it is also about achieving a higher level of personal growth and self-transformation. Under the guidance of a therapist, you can transcend negative patterns, break destructive cycles, and cultivate a healthier, more positive mindset.

Demonstrating Resilience: Seeking professional support is a sign of strength and resilience, not weakness. Recognizing that you need help and taking steps to get it is a courageous step towards self-care and healing. It shows that you value your mental well-being and are willing to invest in your emotional well-being.

A Partnership in the Healing Journey: Collaborating with a therapist is not a solitary experience. It is a partnership in which you are supported by a skilled professional who is committed to your growth and emotional well-being. This partnership can create a safe and supportive environment to explore your emotional wounds, shed old baggage, and move towards a lighter, healthier future.

TECHNIQUES FOR SELF-FORGIVENESS AND FORGIVING OTHERS

Forgiveness is one of the greatest forms of emotional liberation. It does not mean condoning hurtful actions; rather, it involves releasing the emotional burden that such situations carry. Forgiveness grants liberation from resentment and pain, creating space for healing and growth.

Cultivating Self-Compassion

Before embarking on the journey of forgiving others, it is paramount to start with self-forgiveness. Self-compassion is a powerful tool that empowers us to release guilt, shame, and resentment directed towards ourselves. Let us delve deeper into the significance of self-compassion and its effective practice.

Acknowledging Shared Humanity: Self-compassion begins with recognizing that as human beings, we all make mistakes and face challenges. This unites us in a shared humanity, where all have moments of vulnerability, shortcomings, and imperfections. Accepting that you are not the only individual undergoing trials is the first step in cultivating self-compassion.

Treating Yourself with Kindness: Imagine how you would treat a dear friend who is going through a difficult time. You would likely extend kind words, encouragement, and support. Self-compassion means treating yourself in the same way. Instead of harshly criticizing yourself for past mistakes, practice gentle and loving self-talk.

Challenging Destructive Self-Criticism: Self-compassion challenges the destructive self-criticism that often consumes us. Rather than fixating on our failures, mistakes, and imperfections, self-compassion allows us to view these aspects with a softer and more compassionate perspective. Recognize that self-criticism is not constructive; redirect that energy towards nurturing self-love.

Cultivating Unconditional Acceptance: Self-compassion involves unconditionally accepting yourself. This means recognizing your flaws, weaknesses, and challenging moments without judgment. Rather than striving for perpetual perfection, embrace yourself as a constantly evolving human being, deserving of love and respect.

Transcending Shame and Guilt: Shame and guilt can be powerful emotions that keep us tethered to the past. Self-compassion assists in transcending these emotions by acknowledging that we all make mistakes and that these experiences do not define our entirety. Practicing self-compassion enables us to learn from our mistakes instead of becoming ensnared by them.

The Role of Self-Acceptance: Self-compassion is inherently linked to self-acceptance. This means accepting who you are in the present moment, without the need to compare yourself to others or idealized versions of yourself. Self-acceptance forms the foundation upon which self-compassion is built.

The Ongoing Journey of Self-Compassion: The practice of self-compassion is not an ultimate endpoint but rather an ongoing journey. Much like any skill, it requires regular practice to become an integral part of your life. Over time, you will develop a pattern of self-treatment characterized by greater compassion and learn to support yourself during challenging moments.

Self-Compassion and Forgiveness: Self-compassion serves as an essential prerequisite for forgiving others. When you learn to treat yourself with kindness and understanding, you become better equipped to extend that same compassion to others. Forgiveness begins within and ripples outward, impacting your interactions with the world around you.

Cultivating self-compassion is one of the most powerful ways to nurture your sense of self-worth and emotional well-being. This practice transforms the way you perceive and relate to yourself, crafting an inner sanctuary of acceptance, forgiveness, and healing.

Exploring the Essence of Forgiveness

Forgiveness is a profound experience of emotional liberation, resonating deeply for both you and everyone involved. Forgiveness is often misunderstood as forgetting or minimizing the impact of distressing circumstances. However, it is a process of consciously choosing to let go of negativity and resentment associated with such situations. Let's delve further into the significance of forgiveness and how it has the power to transform your life.

A Conscious Choice: Forgiveness is a conscious choice, a deliberate act to free yourself from the shackles of the past. It comes from a place of empowerment, allowing you to take back control of your emotions and no longer be captive to feelings of anger, resentment, or hurt. Forgiveness is a choice you make for yourself, not for the benefit of others.

Unshackling Negativity: When you choose to forgive, you are choosing to let go of the negativity associated with a painful experience. This does not mean negating the impact of what happened; rather, it means choosing not to let that impact continue to control your emotions and your life. Forgiveness is a way to shed the chains that bind you to the past.

A Triumph of Freedom: At its core, the act of forgiveness is an act of liberation. It is emancipation from the emotional prison that binds you to the past. Resentment and anger keep you bound to events that have already happened, preventing you from fully living in the present and creating a more positive future. When you forgive, you choose to break free from these chains and take a step towards inner peace.

Embracing Reality: Forgiveness also involves embracing the reality of what happened. It is not about pretending that others' actions did not have an impact or were harmless. Quite the opposite, it is an acceptance that what happened cannot be changed, but the way you deal with it can be. Forgiveness is an act of embracing the past in order to create a more positive future.

The Forgiveness Process: The forgiveness process is not linear and may take time. It can involve a range of emotions, from initial resistance to acceptance and release. The key is to be gentle with yourself throughout this journey, allowing emotions to arise without judgment. Forgiveness is an act of self-care that requires patience and self-compassion.

The Role of Self-Forgiveness: Before extending forgiveness to others, it is important to practice self-forgiveness. Acknowledge that you are human and capable of making mistakes. At times, we are harder on ourselves than we are on others. Self-forgiveness is an extension of self-compassion, allowing you to free yourself from guilt and self-criticism.

A Transformative Odyssey: Forgiveness is a transformative journey that can liberate you from the emotional burdens of the past and create space for healing and growth. When you choose to forgive, you choose to unshackle yourself from negative emotions that keep you tethered, opening the door to a lighter, more hopeful future. Forgiveness is a gift you give yourself, a path to living with greater freedom and joy.

Embarking on the Path of Forgiveness

Forgiveness is an intimate and personal choice, a decision that only you can make on your own healing journey. It is important to remember that forgiveness does not need to happen instantaneously; rather, it can be a process that unfolds gradually through self-care and time. In this discussion, we will delve further into the art of choosing forgiveness and navigating this journey with understanding and patience.

Acknowledging the Ache and Ire: The first step towards choosing forgiveness is recognizing and validating the emotions that are coursing through you. This often involves confronting the pain, anger, and resentment that have been caused by the situation or person you are considering forgiving. Acknowledging that these emotions are valid and understanding their origin is an essential precursor to beginning the forgiveness process.

Gradually Unleashing Emotions: Forgiveness does not require suppressing or ignoring your emotions; rather, it involves releasing them gradually. It is a journey of allowing emotions to surface and, over time, subside in their intensity. This does not mean forgetting what happened; rather, it emphasizes the choice not to let these negative emotions continue to control your life.

Treading Toward Personal Healing: Forgiveness is an integral part of the tapestry of personal healing. By choosing to forgive, you choose healing over being trapped in the cycle of pain. This includes giving yourself permission to grow, evolve, and create a healthier future. The decision to embrace forgiveness is a testament to your commitment to your own well-being and growth.

The Role of Time in Forgiveness: Time plays an integral role in the forgiveness process. There is no set timeline for when forgiveness must occur. Some wounds may take longer to heal than others. Patience is key. If you are not ready to forgive immediately, that is okay. Allow yourself the necessary time to process your emotions and move towards forgiveness when you are ready.

The Transformation of Forgiveness: The act of choosing forgiveness is a profound transformation. It is a decision that requires courage, empathy, and understanding. When you choose to forgive, you are choosing to let go of the past and create space for a more hopeful future. Remember that forgiveness does not erase what happened; rather, it changes the way you cope with it. It is a journey of self-liberation and personal growth.

Unburdening the Emotional Load

Contemplating the act of forgiveness as a way to unburden yourself of emotional weight is a powerful metaphor that can help you understand the transformative impact of forgiveness on your life. Here is how this metaphor can be applied and how it is inherently linked to creating a lighter existence filled with self-love.

The Metaphor of Emotional Weight: Imagine the resentment, anger, and pain you hold onto as emotional weights that you carry. Over time, these weights can accumulate and become a burden that affects your energy, peace of mind, and ability to live fully. The act of forgiveness is like releasing these weights, one by one, allowing you to feel unshackled and free.

Releasing into Lightness: Viewing forgiveness as an act of releasing emotional weight can evoke a profound sense of relief. Imagine that through forgiveness, you are unshackling yourself from these emotional burdens that have weighed you down. As you release them, you feel lighter, as if a burden has been lifted from your shoulders. This sensation of lightness is indicative of the inner space that forgiveness creates.

Journeying Toward a Lighter Life: Forgiveness not only unburdens you of the emotional weight of the past, but it also creates space for a lighter and more joyful life in the present and future. By letting go of the emotional baggage of resentment and anger, you make room for positive emotions like peace, gratitude, and joy. You liberate yourself from toxic emotions that have held you captive and begin to experience a new sense of emotional freedom.

Self-Love and Emotional Liberation: The act of unburdening yourself of emotional weight through forgiveness is deeply connected to self-love. When you choose to forgive, you are demonstrating love and compassion for yourself. You are prioritizing your emotional well-being and health over the need to hold onto resentments. This choice is a testament to your commitment to your own happiness and growth.

A Fresh Perspective: Picturing forgiveness as a liberation from emotional weight can also help you adopt a new outlook on the situation or person you are forgiving. Instead of dwelling on past pain, you can begin to see forgiveness as an opportunity to create a more positive and fulfilling future. This shift in perspective can be liberating and empowering.

Cultivating Empathy

Empathy is a precious skill that allows us to see the world through the eyes of others, understanding their perspectives, feelings, and circumstances. In the realm of forgiveness, nurturing empathy can play a pivotal role in unburdening emotional baggage and facilitating the process of forgiveness. Here's how empathy can serve as a powerful tool to pave the way for both forgiveness and self-love.

Understanding Diverse Perspectives: A fundamental aspect of empathy is earnestly striving to understand the viewpoints of others. This does not mean agreeing with their actions or justifying harmful behavior; rather, it means comprehending the factors that may have contributed to their choices. Sometimes, one's actions may be influenced by their own struggles and emotional wounds.

Acknowledging Emotional Baggage: Each of us carries our own emotional baggage, composed of past experiences, traumas, and personal challenges. Cultivating empathy entails recognizing that, just like ourselves, others also grapple with internal struggles. This does not diminish the significance of our own experiences, but it helps to forge a deeper, more humane connection with others.

Constructing Bridges of Understanding: By practicing empathy, we are constructing bridges of understanding between ourselves and others. This can create a space where we begin to realize the shared humanity and underlying similarities we all possess. Empathy not only promotes understanding, but also helps reduce hostility and anger, thus facilitating the process of forgiveness.

Empathy and Relationship Reframing: Cultivating empathy can be particularly beneficial when forgiving someone with whom we have had a complicated relationship. By understanding this person's perspectives and experiences, we may start to view the relationship in a more comprehensive and holistic light. This can enable us to redefine the relationship in a manner that is healthier for both parties.

Compassion and Self-Care: In addition to aiding forgiveness towards others, empathy is also a tool for nurturing self-love. When we practice self-empathy, we are tending to our own struggles and challenges with kindness and compassion. This fosters an internal environment of self-care and acceptance.

The Path to Healing

The process of releasing emotional baggage is a journey of profound healing and personal transformation. It involves delving into the depths of your emotions, confronting past traumas, and ultimately allowing yourself to release the emotional weight that has kept you captive. In this discussion, we will delve into the path of healing with meticulous scrutiny, spotlighting the pivotal components that constitute this voyage of inner growth.

Courage to Confront the Wounds: The healing journey begins with the courage to confront the emotional wounds you have borne. This involves looking back and acknowledging the poignant experiences that have shaped your beliefs, behaviors, and emotions. It is an act of courage to squarely face these wounds, allowing yourself to feel the pain and sorrow entangled with them.

Acceptance and Insight: As you delve into your emotional wounds, it is imperative to cultivate acceptance and insight. This means recognizing that past experiences have molded who you are today, but they do not define your future. Embracing the struggles of yesteryear and understanding how they have influenced you is a pivotal step on the path to healing.

Kindness and Self-Forgiveness: The healing journey also encompasses being kind to oneself and practicing self-forgiveness. This means relinquishing self-criticism and acknowledging that you deserve the same compassion that you extend to others. By forgiving yourself for past choices and the difficult emotions you have weathered, you carve out space for profound healing.

Forgiveness as a Shortcut to Healing: Forgiveness is one of the quickest ways to emotional healing. When you choose to forgive yourself and others, you release the negativity that has ensnared you. Forgiveness is like detaching an emotional anchor that had been holding you back. It creates room for growth, transformation, and connection with self-love.

An Avenue for Flourishing: By unburdening emotional weight and traversing the path of healing, you are creating an avenue for self-love to flourish. With negativity expelled, there is room for feelings of peace, joy, and inner acceptance. You become acutely aware of your identity and the boundless potential you possess to forge a purposeful life.

Growth and Emotional Connection: The healing process is not confined to the past; it also pertains to the future. As you heal, you unlock doors to new opportunities for personal growth and emotional connection. You are laying a sturdy foundation for healthier relationships, authenticity, and a profound sense of well-being.

An Unceasing Odyssey: The journey of healing is an endless odyssey, for life is in perpetual evolution. As you ascend, new layers of emotions and experiences may surface. The key is to use the tools you have gathered along the way to continue releasing emotional baggage and foster self-love in every facet of your life.

Releasing emotional baggage is an act of self-love and self-empowerment. By confronting past traumas, shattering negative patterns, and embracing forgiveness, you are paving the way for profound growth and positive transformation. This paves the way for a more authentic life, healthier relationships, and a lighter heart. As you liberate the past, you unfold into the present, creating a brighter future.

CHAPTER 6
CRAFTING WHOLESOME RELATIONSHIPS

Erecting bridges of self-love
for relationships that mirror
your essence.

Healthy relationships are the foundation of a fulfilling and joyous life. They provide us with support, love, connection, and a sense of belonging. In this chapter, we will explore the nuances of wholesome relationships, from nurturing their inception to sustaining them over time. We will learn the art of tending to relationships that contribute to our emotional well-being and personal growth.

DISCERNING THE PILLARS OF A WHOLESOME RELATIONSHIP

A wholesome relationship is like a sturdy edifice, built upon pillars that support the connection and mutual growth of the partners. Let us delve into each of these pillars in depth, to understand how they contribute to the foundation of thriving relationships:

Open Communication and Honesty

Picture a relationship as a bridge that links two souls. This bridge is upheld by essential pillars, anchoring it firmly and securely, allowing the partners' connection to flourish. One of these pillars is open communication and honesty. These two pillars combine to create a strong and profound relationship, empowering partners to understand, support, and grow alongside each other. Let us examine in detail how open communication and honesty form the foundation of this bridge:

Open Communication, the Bastion of Mutual Understanding: Open communication is the bedrock, like a bridge's foundation. It creates space for partners to express themselves freely, sharing their emotions, thoughts, and needs. When the channels of communication are open, there is a sense of security in knowing that you can express yourself without fear of judgment. Open communication goes beyond speech alone; it also encompasses attentive listening to one another. This underscores respect and a genuine interest in the partner's perspective.

Open communication is especially valuable when it comes to conflict resolution. When partners feel comfortable expressing their concerns and emotions, misunderstandings can be cleared up and issues resolved constructively. The absence of open communication can breed unspoken resentments and exacerbate conflicts that could have been avoided through candid dialogue.

Honesty, the Adhesive Upholding the Bridge's Strength: Think of honesty as the adhesive that holds the bridge's components together. Honesty is essential in building and maintaining trust between partners. When you are candid about your emotions, experiences, and expectations, you lay a firm foundation of mutual trust. Trust is the cornerstone of any healthy relationship; it is the conduit through which partners open up emotionally, feel secure, and foster a genuine connection.

Honesty is also essential in preventing misunderstandings and conflicts. By being transparent about your thoughts and feelings, you can avoid the construction of faulty assumptions or distorted interpretations. This can prevent many misunderstandings and keep communication flowing smoothly.

The Symphony of Open Communication and Honesty: Open communication and honesty harmonize like a symphony in a relationship. Open communication is the melody that allows partners to voice, share, and connect emotionally. Honesty is the rhythm that sustains this melody's cohesion and balance. When partners communicate openly and honestly with each other, they are building a strong foundation to face challenges and enjoy the joys that life together reveals.

In a relationship that values open communication and honesty, partners feel understood, respected, and supported. They know that they can rely on each other to share their triumphs and tribulations. They can face challenges together, knowing that open communication and honesty are the tools that will guide them through any obstacle.

Mutual Reverence and Empathy

Imagine a relationship as a meticulously tended garden. The soil in which this garden thrives is composed of two vital components: mutual reverence and empathy. These elements are akin to fertile soil, fostering the blossoming of the relationship, creating an ambiance of love, understanding, and support. Let us delve into the significance of mutual reverence and empathy in detail:

Mutual Reverence, the Bedrock of Connection: Reverence serves as the resolute foundation upon which a healthy relationship is built. Each individual is recognized as unique and invaluable. This signifies not only accepting the partner's individuality but also cherishing their opinions, sentiments, and desires. When reverence is present, both partners feel secure in their authenticity, knowing their voices are heard and respected.

Reverence extends beyond mere words; it manifests through consistent actions. This entails treating one's partner with consideration, not belittling their viewpoints, and establishing healthy boundaries. Reverence engenders an atmosphere of trust and security, where both can express their needs and expectations without fear of judgment.

Empathy, the Bridge to Profound Connection: Imagine empathy as a bridge connecting the hearts and minds of partners. Empathy embodies the capacity to step into the other's shoes, comprehending their perspectives, feelings, and experiences. When you practice empathy, you are displaying a profound reverence for your partner's inner world. This forges a potent emotional connection, where both feel genuinely understood.

Empathy is also a potent tool for conflict resolution. When you endeavor to fathom your partner's emotions and motivations, you can discover solutions that cater to both parties' needs. Empathy aids in forestalling the escalation of conflicts, as it fosters a secure space for honest and vulnerable expression.

The Harmonious Dance Between Reverence and Empathy: Mutual reverence and empathy engage in a harmonious dance between partners. Reverence lays the firm foundation for connection, while empathy constructs emotional bridges between them. With both elements in place, the relationship transforms into a space where partners can grow individually and as a unit.

Practicing mutual reverence and empathy demands continuous attention and effort. This encompasses active listening, validating the partner's feelings, and genuinely showing interest in their experiences. It also involves patience and understanding when challenges arise.

Crafting a Sanctuary of Love and Understanding: When mutual reverence and empathy are cultivated within a relationship, it metamorphoses into a sanctuary of love and understanding. Partners feel secure in sharing their joys and concerns, confident they will be valued and comprehended. They celebrate each other's victories and stand by each other in times of difficulty.

Mutual reverence and empathy also facilitate partners' individual growth as well as growth as a couple. They lay a sturdy foundation for navigating life's challenges together, secure in the knowledge that they have an unwavering supporter by their side. As the soil of mutual reverence and empathy is nurtured, the relationship's garden flourishes into a landscape of love, trust, and authentic connection.

Trust and Support

Imagine a relationship as the construction of a grand estate. Trust stands as the bedrock supporting the entire structure, while support resembles the intricate network of beams and columns that uphold it. Let us delve into the significance of trust and support within a relationship and how they intertwine to forge an enduring and resilient bond.

Erecting Trust, the Foundation of Connection: Trust is not an instant edifice, but rather a masterpiece crafted over time through consistent actions, open communication, and mutual respect. It embodies the unwavering belief that your partner will honor their commitments and stand beside you, regardless of circumstances. Trust transcends mere faithfulness; it encompasses the confidence that they will be there to buoy you emotionally, to share in your concerns, and to confront challenges side by side.

Once fractured, trust can prove a challenge to rebuild. Hence, maintaining integrity, being transparent, and upholding promises are all vital. Trust flourishes when words and actions align, when secrets find no refuge, and when both partners are committed to preserving each other's trust.

Support, the Beams Sustaining the Relationship: Support mirrors the beams and columns that underpin the relationship's structure. It extends beyond words of encouragement, encompassing emotional and practical sustenance. Emotional support entails being present for your partner when they most need it: proffering a comforting shoulder, listening with empathy, and exchanging genuine sentiments. Emotional support creates an environment wherein both partners feel accepted and cherished, even amidst hardship.

Practical support, in turn, entails acting in the relationship's best interest. This may entail helping with daily tasks, championing your partner's dreams and aspirations, or collaborating to overcome obstacles. Practical support showcases your commitment to mutual growth and your willingness to collaborate to forge a better life together.

The Symbiosis of Trust and Support: Trust and support are inextricably intertwined. Trust forms the foundation upon which support is built, while support fortifies trust by demonstrating your steadfast presence regardless of circumstance. When trust is shaken, support is essential to help rebuild it. Likewise, when support is needed, trust provides the assurance that both partners can seek solace in each other without hesitation.

The marriage of trust and support creates an environment where partners can be both vulnerable and authentic. They have the confidence that they can rely on each other to overcome challenges and celebrate triumphs. When the pillars of trust and support stand tall, the relationship becomes a wellspring of security, love, and personal growth. It is a shared journey, where both partners lift each other up to build a profoundly meaningful life together.

Defining Healthy Boundaries

Picture a healthy relationship as an exquisitely designed mansion. Healthy boundaries are the walls that delineate and safeguard individual spaces, while also fostering the connection between partners. Let us delve into how the establishment of healthy boundaries is paramount to upholding a relationship that is both respectful and harmonious.

Boundaries, Where Individuality Flourishes: Just as each person is unique, so are their needs, desires, and personal spaces. Establishing healthy boundaries involves understanding and clearly articulating where your individuality ends and your partner's begins. This not only cultivates mutual respect but also safeguards the identity of each.

Having healthy boundaries is a way of asserting self-love and self-respect. It involves recognizing your own emotional, physical, and mental needs and openly communicating them to your partner. By establishing boundaries, you are demonstrating your willingness to protect yourself and preserve your identity, even within the confines of the relationship.

Building Bridges, Not Walls: The definition of healthy boundaries does not mean erecting walls that isolate you from your partner. On the contrary, it is about constructing bridges of communication and understanding. When both partners understand and honor each other's boundaries, it creates an environment where both can feel at ease to be authentic and vulnerable.

Setting boundaries also prevents needless conflict. When both know the extent to which they can go without causing hurt feelings, misunderstandings diminish, and differences are addressed sensitively. This fosters an atmosphere of security and trust, where both can grow individually and as a couple.

Respecting the Partner's Individuality: Having healthy boundaries is an expression of respect for your partner's individuality. It signifies acknowledging that each possesses their own needs and limits, and that these differences should not only be accepted, but cherished. By setting and respecting each other's boundaries, you are nurturing a relationship grounded in acceptance and genuine love.

Defining healthy boundaries is an ongoing process. As you and your partner evolve and grow, it is important to review and adjust boundaries as needed. This demonstrates your commitment to maintaining a healthy, harmonious relationship where both can thrive individually and as a couple. When the walls of boundaries are constructed with respect and love, they evolve into the bedrock of a lasting and meaningful relationship.

Sharing Values and Aspirations

Envision a relationship as akin to a grand edifice. The foundation, the walls, and now the roof, symbolizing unity through shared values and aspirations. Let us embark upon the exploration of how common values and goals are the bedrock of a healthy and enduring relationship.

Erecting a Roof of Compatibility: Just as a roof provides shelter from the elements, sharing values and aspirations offers an emotional haven within the relationship. Having a sturdy bedrock of shared beliefs and objectives constructs a framework that guides both partners toward a shared future. While each remains a distinct individual, this unified foundation is an essential element in maintaining connection and harmony.

It's important to recognize that sharing values does not mean complete agreement on all matters. On the contrary, it is about acknowledging core beliefs that steer your decisions and actions. This sows fertile ground for mutual understanding and conflict resolution, as both are aligned in their trajectory.

Influence in Decision-Making: Just as a roof shield against weathering, compatibility in values guards against divergent choices. When both partners share fundamental values, they can navigate significant decisions with greater harmony. This helps to avert conflicts that may arise due to fundamental differences in perspective.

Moreover, having shared values and objectives provides a scaffold for conflict resolution. When differences surface, both can turn back to these shared values to find solutions that are mutually satisfying. This engenders an atmosphere of cooperation and respect, rather than competition or confrontation.

Growing Together Over Time: As time unfolds, relationships evolve and transform. Shared values and aspirations assist the relationship in growing in positive directions. Both partners possess a clear vision of what they aim to achieve together and are committed to bolstering each other's growth. This not only maintains emotional connection but also nurtures a shared sense of purpose.

Sharing values and aspirations not only fortifies the bond but also contributes to individual and collective fulfillment. When you mutually support each other in the pursuit of shared aspirations, you create an environment of love and support, where both can flourish. Just as a roof shields a house, sharing values and aspirations safeguards and enriches the emotional bond you share with one another.

Constructive Conflict Resolution

Envision conflicts as passing storms that test the resilience of a dwelling. Constructive conflict resolution is the strategy to fortify the walls of your relationship, ensuring its steadfastness and security.

Intermittent Storms and the Power of Constructive Resolution: Just as storms gauge the stability of a structure, conflicts test the strength of a relationship. Conflicts are inherent in any coexistence, and constructive resolution is the approach that transforms challenges into opportunities for growth. It involves a partnership mindset, where both partners commit to attentive listening and comprehension of each other's perspectives.

The Power of Attentive Listening: Listening forms the bedrock of constructive resolution. When both partners strive to listen actively and empathetically, they carve space for mutual understanding. This involves not merely hearing words, but grasping underlying emotions. Attentive listening demonstrates respect and fosters a safe environment where both can voice concerns.

Expressing Concerns with Respect: Just as a dwelling necessitates regular maintenance, relationships too require periodic reviews. Articulating concerns with respect is a way to uphold the health of the relationship. This involves communicating without criticism or blame, focusing on actions and feelings rather than pointing fingers. Nonviolent and respectful communication maintains the integrity of relationship walls.

Collaboratively Seeking Solutions: Constructive conflict resolution is a collaborative, not competitive, approach. Both partners are willing to find solutions that cater to both, rather than striving to prove who is right. This entails the readiness to compromise, seek middle grounds, and discover ways to surmount challenges together. Collaborative conflict resolution reinforces the foundations of the relationship.

Cultivating Patience and Empathy: Just as a dwelling requires constant upkeep, relationships also demand ongoing effort. Patience is paramount during conflict resolution, as not all problems are instantly resolved. Empathy is the tool that enables you to see the situation from the other's perspective, engendering deeper connection and mutual understanding.

Enduring Benefits of Constructive Resolution: Constructive conflict resolution not only addresses immediate issues but also forges enduring trust and understanding. When both partners confront challenges together in a respectful and collaborative manner, it reinforces the structure of the relationship. Constructively resolved conflicts metamorphose into opportunities for personal and mutual growth, strengthening the relationship walls to withstand any storm.

The pillars of a healthy relationship comprise the solid foundation upon which you build a profound and meaningful connection. Each pillar is pivotal and interconnected, and together, they work in concert to uphold the relationship over time. By comprehending and nurturing these pillars, you invest in the growth and prosperity of the relationship, rendering it more resilient against any challenges that may arise.

HOW SELF-LOVE INFLUENCES PARTNER SELECTION

Self-love is like a filter that directly shapes the choice of partners. When you foster a healthy relationship with yourself, you are more likely to make decisions that honor your happiness and well-being. Here are some ways in which self-love influences your choice of partners:

Self-Knowledge

Imagine self-knowledge as the compass that guides your voyage across the seas of relationships. The deeper your understanding of yourself, the clearer the path you will want to take in the waters of intimacy and connection.

The Journey of Inner Exploration: Self-knowledge is an inward journey that demands a willingness to delve into all facets of who you are. It is like charting a map of your own mind, heart, and soul. What are your deepest passions? What core values guide your choices? What are your dreams and boundaries? The deeper you venture, the more you will unearth about your true identity.

The Mirror of Self-Love: Self-love is the mirror that reflects your authentic essence. When you have a healthy relationship with yourself, you can discern your desires and needs with clarity. This mirror reflects back qualities that are important to you in a relationship, such as respect, open communication, and mutual support.

Nurturing self-love is like polishing this mirror, ensuring that it accurately reflects who you are and what you seek.

Recognizing Compatibility and Incompatibility: When you cultivate a strong relationship with yourself, you become better equipped to recognize compatibility with a potential partner. You can discern whether your passions and values align, if there is a genuine emotional connection, and if the relationship contributes to your personal growth. At the same time, you become more attuned to signs of incompatibility and harmful patterns.

Laying the Foundation of a Relationship: When you build a solid foundation of self-love, you establish the bedrock for a healthy relationship. You do not enter a relationship to fill emotional voids or seek external validation. Instead, you join a partner to share love, growth, and joy. Self-love helps you set healthy boundaries and choose partners who cherish your authenticity.

The Guiding Beacon: Imagine your course through the sea of relationships guided by a beacon. This beacon is self-knowledge, shining brightly over uncertain waters. It directs you in choosing partners who will navigate alongside you toward a shared horizon. The stronger this beacon of self-love, the more clearly you will perceive the contours of relationships that are truly enriching and aligned with who you are.

Avoiding Toxic Relationships

Imagine self-love as an internal compass that guides you through the complex and often nebulous terrain of relationships. This compass is essential for identifying and avoiding toxic relationships, helping you to stay on the right course and safeguard your emotional well-being.

Discerning Toxicity: Self-love is like a pair of special spectacles that allow you to clearly see the signs of toxic relationships. You are attuned to your own emotions and needs, which means you can detect when something is amiss. These special spectacles empower you to see beyond the surface, identifying behavior patterns that may be detrimental in the long run.

Connection with Your Intuition: With self-love, you fortify your connection with your intuition. This wise inner voice often signals when something is awry in a relationship. You learn to trust your intuition and recognize feelings of discomfort that can signify a toxic environment. This intimate connection with your intuition is like a shield that safeguards you against relationships that could harm your happiness and well-being.

The Courage to Walk Away: Self-love grants you the courage to walk away from relationships that do not value you or that are detrimental. You understand that you deserve to be treated with respect, empathy, and support. This deeply ingrained understanding bolsters your ability to say "no" to situations that do not align with your values and needs. You do not compromise your self-esteem in exchange for a relationship that fails to meet your expectations.

Setting Strong Boundaries: Having self-love means you establish firm boundaries to protect your emotional well-being. You do not allow anyone to cross these boundaries, even if it means having to distance yourself from an unhealthy relationship. Having clear boundaries is a direct expression of self-love, as it demonstrates that you prioritize your own well-being.

Prioritizing Your Well-Being: Self-love places your well-being at the forefront. This means you refuse to remain in a relationship that consistently drains your energy, undermines your self-confidence, or makes you question your own worth. Self-love signifies that you are the guardian of your own happiness and are willing to take steps to keep it intact.

Choosing Nourishing Relationships: With self-love, you choose relationships that nurture your soul. You seek partners who value you, support your goals, and share a healthy emotional environment. You recognize that you deserve a relationship where your authenticity is celebrated, your emotions are respected, and your growth is encouraged.

As you navigate the waters of life with self-love, you protect your inner peace, strengthen your self-esteem, and ensure that your relationships are sources of joy, growth, and mutual respect.

Selecting Compatible Partners

When it comes to selecting compatible partners, self-love acts as a reliable guide, directing you towards relationships that truly add value to your life. Self-love is the solid foundation upon which you build the pillars of a healthy and enduring relationship.

Esteeming Healthy Relationships: Rooted in self-love, you hold in high regard relationships built upon mutual respect, trust, and growth. Instead of seeking external validation, you pursue a partnership that contributes to your emotional well-being and supports your life goals. Self-love enables you to recognize that you deserve a relationship that celebrates who you are, rather than attempting to fill emotional voids or insecurities.

The Quest for Profound Compatibility: Self-love hones your ability to seek compatibility on deep levels. You're not merely interested in superficialities but are in search of someone with whom you share fundamental values, goals, and aspirations. This longing for profound compatibility is a reflection of self-love, as it signifies your unwillingness to settle for relationships that do not align with your true essence.

Elevating the Standard of Relationships: Self-love raises your standard when it comes to relationships. You don't settle for less than you deserve and are willing to wait for the right partner, rather than contenting yourself with someone who doesn't meet your emotional and personal needs. Having self-love allows you to understand that you deserve a relationship that enriches your life and contributes to your ongoing growth.

Focus on Mutual Growth: When choosing compatible partners, you're more interested in mutual growth than mere validation. Self-love grants you the clarity to understand that a healthy relationship is not about finding someone to fill all your gaps, but about finding someone with whom you can grow, learn, and evolve together. You seek a partner who positively challenges you and is committed to a process of continuous growth.

Avoiding Need-Based Relationships: With self-love, you can avoid the trap of entering relationships out of sheer emotional necessity. Instead of seeking someone to "complete you," you seek someone who complements your journey and enriches your life. This means you don't rush into relationships out of loneliness or neediness, but rather make conscious decisions based on what truly contributes to your happiness and well-being.

Choosing compatible partners with self-love not only strengthens your self-esteem, but it also lays the groundwork for relationships that are enriching, respectful, and fulfilling. Self-love is the key to building a future of love and well-being, where your choices are guided by your ability to recognize and value what truly matters in a relationship.

Establishing Clear Boundaries

In relationships, setting healthy boundaries is a direct expression of self-love. Having a clear understanding of who you are and what you need empowers you to set limits that safeguard your emotional well-being and honor your individuality.

Preserving Individuality: Self-love allows you to recognize that you are a unique individual, with distinct needs, desires, and boundaries. Establishing healthy boundaries is a way to protect your individuality, ensuring that you don't forfeit who you are for the sake of the relationship. This creates a balance where you can share your life with someone without losing your identity.

Respecting Your Own Needs: Self-love means valuing your own needs as much as you value your partner's. By setting clear boundaries, you communicate your emotional, physical, and mental needs. This ensures that your needs are not overlooked, and you are nurturing yourself while investing in the relationship.

Assertive Communication: Self-love is foundational for assertive communication. You understand that your voice and opinions matter and deserve to be heard. By setting boundaries, you are communicating your limits in a respectful and assertive manner, allowing your partner to understand your expectations and avoid future misunderstandings.

Realistic Expectations: With self-love, you enter a relationship with realistic expectations. You know what you are willing to accept and what you are not. This establishes a firm foundation for the relationship from the outset, preventing disagreements down the road. Having clear boundaries also helps avoid breeding resentments due to unmet expectations.

Preventing Unnecessary Conflicts: Establishing healthy boundaries is an effective way to prevent unnecessary conflicts. By clearly defining your limits and needs, you are setting the rules of engagement. This can reduce the likelihood of misunderstandings or accidentally crossing boundaries, which often lead to conflicts.

Promoting Mutual Respect: Healthy boundaries are an expression of mutual respect. They demonstrate that you respect both your own needs and expectations, as well as those of your partner. When both partners have clear boundaries, it creates an environment of respect, understanding, and mutual consideration, strengthening the emotional connection.

Setting healthy boundaries is an act of self-love that fortifies the relationship while safeguarding your own emotional well-being. With self-love as your guide, you can cultivate a relationship where both parties feel valued, respected, and supported on their individual and shared journeys.

Embracing Authenticity

Authenticity is like the light that illuminates a relationship, revealing its true and unique colors. Self-love holds the key to nurturing and preserving this authenticity, enabling you and your partner to engage in a genuine and meaningful manner.

Freedom to Be Your True Self: When you love yourself, you don't have to hide your true self. This means you have the freedom to share your thoughts, emotions, and aspirations without fear of judgment or rejection. Authenticity thrives when you feel comfortable being your true self, including your vulnerabilities and idiosyncrasies.

Abandoning the Need for Approval: Self-love liberates you from the trap of trying to please at any cost. You don't need to change your personality, interests, or values to fit your partner's expectations. Instead, you value authenticity and seek a relationship where both partners support and embrace each other as they are.

Genuine Connections: Authentic relationships are characterized by genuine connections. When you and your partner are both authentic, you are sharing genuine parts of yourselves. This creates a deeper connection, as you both feel truly known and understood. Authenticity nurtures emotional intimacy and strengthens bonds.

Appreciating Diversity: Self-love helps you value and respect diversity within the relationship. Your partner does not need to mirror you in every way. Rather, you appreciate individual differences and see these differences as opportunities for mutual learning and growth.

Preventing Resentment: Being authentic prevents the buildup of resentment. When you hide parts of yourself or act contrary to your values, it can lead to feelings of frustration and hurt. Authenticity prevents the buildup of such resentments, as you are open and honest from the outset.

Cultivating Trust: Authenticity is the foundation of trust. When you are authentic, you demonstrate trustworthiness by not hiding anything from your partner. This builds mutual trust, allowing both of you to feel secure in being yourselves and sharing your most intimate thoughts and feelings.

Cultivating authenticity in a relationship is an act of self-love that benefits both you and your partner. When both of you can truly be yourselves, the relationship evolves into a space of growth, profound connection, and unconditional acceptance. Self-love is the key that unlocks the door to an authentic and meaningful relationship.

Seeking Complementary Relationships

When it comes to relationships, the pursuit of complementary bonds is a reflection of self-love and a profound understanding of your own needs and values. Here's a deeper look at how self-love influences the quest for complementary relationships:

Completing, Not Filling: Self-love means that you don't enter a relationship seeking to fill emotional voids. Instead, you seek a partner who complements your life in a positive way. You already have a sense of wholeness within yourself and want to share your journey with someone who can add value and joy to your life.

Mutual Growth and Support: Complementary relationships are rooted in mutual growth. When you love yourself, you want to be with someone who challenges you to expand and evolve. You see the relationship as an opportunity for learning and enrichment, where both partners can support and encourage each other in their aspirations and goals.

Values–Based Connections: Self-love influences you to seek a partner who shares similar core values. This creates a solid foundation for the relationship, as both partners are aligned in terms of ethics, goals, and life visions. Complementary relationships are built on the sturdy pillars of shared values.

Independence and Intimacy: The pursuit of complementary relationships is a mark of emotional maturity and self-love. You understand the importance of maintaining your independence and identity even as you share your life with someone. This allows both partners to enjoy moments of intimacy and deep connection while respecting each other's space and individuality.

Reducing Unrealistic Expectations: When you love yourself, you're less likely to place unrealistic expectations on the relationship or your partner. You don't expect the other person to be responsible for your happiness or to fill all the gaps in your life. This reduces pressure on the relationship and creates a space where both partners can feel comfortable being authentic.

Harmony and Well-Being: Complementary relationships result in an overall sense of well-being and harmony. You don't feel emotionally overwhelmed or drained by the relationship, as both partners are positively contributing to each other's well-being. The presence of self-love enables you to choose a partner who enhances your happiness rather than depleting it.

Seeking complementary relationships is an expression of the respect and love you have for yourself. This approach leads to balanced, nurturing, and enriching relationships where both partners can grow individually and together. Self-love serves as the compass guiding you toward a relationship that enriches your life and brings genuine joy.

Contribution to a Healthy Relationship

Self-love plays a pivotal role in how you contribute to a healthy relationship. Here are some ways that self-love can influence your engagement in a relationship:

Sharing Love, Not Seeking Validation: When you have self-love, you enter a relationship not to seek validation or fill emotional voids, but to share your love and joy. You don't place the responsibility of your self-esteem in your partner's hands; instead, you share your unconditional love and positivity.

Fostering Mutual Growth: Self-love empowers you to be a partner who contributes to mutual growth. You seek not only personal growth, but also encourage and support your partner's growth. This creates an environment where both partners can learn, evolve, and become the best versions of themselves.

Shared Responsibility for Happiness: Self-love leads you to understand that happiness is not solely your partner's responsibility. You recognize the importance of maintaining your own happiness and well-being, rather than depending solely on the relationship for it. This lessens pressure on your partner and cultivates an atmosphere of mutual emotional support.

Balance in Giving and Receiving: Self-love allows you to find a healthy equilibrium between giving and receiving in the relationship. You don't lose yourself in sacrificing your needs to fulfill your partner's, nor do you expect your partner to do the same. This establishes a dynamic where both partners have space to grow individually and share moments of togetherness.

Promoting Self-Acceptance: When you love yourself, you're more likely to promote self-acceptance within your relationship. You're willing to accept your partner for who they are, without attempting to change them to fit your own expectations. This creates a space where both partners can be authentic and genuine with each other.

Self-care for Relationship Care: Self-love involves ongoing self-care, both emotionally and physically. Taking care of yourself ensures that you're in a healthy emotional and mental state to contribute positively to the relationship. This helps prevent emotional exhaustion and

fosters the ability to handle relationship challenges constructively.

Communication and Vulnerability: Self-love also
plays a role in how you communicate and open up within
a relationship. When you love yourself, you're more willing to be vulnerable and share your feelings, thoughts,
and fears with your partner. This fosters an environment
of trust and intimacy, where both partners can connect on
a deeper level.

Building healthy relationships takes a continuous investment of love, respect, and communication. When you
have self-love, you're more likely to choose partners who
complement your life rather than complete it. Remember
that the relationship starts with you - the more you love
yourself, the more capable you are of forging connections
that nurture your growth and emotional well-being.

CHAPTER 7

SETTING BOUNDARIES AND SAYING "NO"

Set boundaries with self-love
and decline with the might
a strong heart.

Setting boundaries and expressing "no" are essential skills for taking care of your emotional, mental, and physical well-being. In this chapter, we will explore the importance of setting healthy limits in different areas of life, understand why saying no is a form of self-care, and discuss strategies for effectively communicating your boundaries.

THE IMPORTANCE OF SETTING BOUNDARIES TO PROTECT YOUR SELF-ESTEEM

Imagine your boundaries as the banks of a river that protect its inner waters. Similarly, setting boundaries is a practice that protects your self-esteem and emotional well-being. When you establish clear boundaries, you are communicating to yourself and others what is acceptable and respectful in terms of behavior, interactions, and expectations. Here are some reasons why setting boundaries is important for preserving your self-esteem:

Recognition of Your Own Worth

The process of setting boundaries goes far beyond simply erecting physical or emotional barriers. It is deeply rooted in the recognition of your own self-worth and the awareness of what you deserve as a unique and valuable human being. By setting boundaries, you are sending a clear message to the world and to yourself: "I deserve respect and I am worthy of considerate treatment."

Self-Compassion as the Foundation: Recognizing one's own worth is intertwined with self-compassion, which is the practice of treating oneself with kindness and compassion, just as you would treat a dear friend. When you acknowledge your own limits and communicate them assertively, you are practicing self-compassion by prioritizing your own needs and well-being.

Impact on Self-Esteem: Allowing others to overstep your boundaries can have a detrimental impact on your self-esteem. It can make you feel devalued, inadequate, and even invisible. On the other hand, establishing healthy boundaries fosters a sense of dignity and self-worth. When you stand up against situations that do not respect your limits, you are protecting your self-esteem and maintaining a sense of integrity.

The Relationship Between Boundaries and Empowerment: Setting boundaries is also an act of personal empowerment. It allows you to take control over situations in your life and choose how you want to be treated. When you set boundaries, you are affirming your own power to make decisions and shape your interactions. This results in a greater sense of control over your own life and well-being.

Breaking Old Patterns: For many people, setting boundaries represents a departure from old patterns of behavior. It may involve overcoming deeply ingrained beliefs that you must always please others or sacrifice your own needs to be accepted. By recognizing your own worth and setting boundaries, you are challenging these old patterns and creating a new paradigm based on self-respect.

Setting boundaries is not just about protecting yourself from negative situations; it is also an assertion of self-love and personal worth. By acknowledging that you deserve to be treated with respect and dignity, you are creating an environment that nurtures your self-esteem, emotional well-being, and personal growth. The ongoing practice of establishing healthy boundaries is an act of self-compassion that honors your own uniqueness and contributes to a more balanced and fulfilling life.

Shielding Against Exploitation and Abuse

Establishing healthy boundaries is a fundamental line of defense against exploitation, manipulation, and abuse by others. When you set clear boundaries, you are delineating the territory in which you feel secure, respected, and valued. This is particularly important when it comes to personal, professional, and even social relationships. How healthy boundaries provide protection against exploitation and abuse:

Empowerment and Recognition of Worth: By setting boundaries, you are affirming your own worth and dignity. This sends a clear message that you will not tolerate behaviors that violate your integrity and well-being. This empowered stance serves as a natural deterrent to those who might attempt to exploit or abuse you.

Identification of Inappropriate Behavior: Setting boundaries helps you promptly identify inappropriate behavior. When you know your own limits, you can recognize when someone is unfairly or harmfully crossing those boundaries. This gives you the ability to intervene immediately and protect yourself from any potential exploitation.

Resistance to Manipulation: Manipulative individuals often target those who struggle to set boundaries. In doing so, they seek to exploit the person's willingness to accommodate their own needs. However, when you are adept at establishing clear boundaries, you become less susceptible to manipulation, as you do not allow others to influence you to act contrary to your desires or values.

Reinforcement of Autonomy: Healthy boundaries promote your personal autonomy. You are making informed decisions about what is acceptable to you and what is not. This ensures that you are in control of your actions and choices, rather than being manipulated by external influences. When you hold the power to set boundaries, you are safeguarding your independence.

Emotional and Mental Protection: Exploitation and abuse are not confined solely to the physical realm. They can also occur emotionally and mentally. Setting boundaries helps protect your mental and emotional well-being, ensuring that you are not subject to behaviors that could harm your self-esteem, confidence, or psychological welfare.

Establishing healthy boundaries is an essential part of safeguarding your emotional, mental, and physical well-being. By defining your own limits, you position yourself as the guardian of your own integrity. This provides protection against any exploitation, manipulation, or abuse that may arise in various areas of your life. By maintaining your boundaries, you demonstrate that your self-esteem and self-valuation take precedence, creating an environment where you are treated with respect and dignity.

Fortifying Self-Trust

The consistent practice of setting and maintaining healthy boundaries not only shields you against exploitation and abuse, but also plays a pivotal role in fortifying self-trust. This process of empowerment contributes to a positive self-image and a sense of self-efficacy. Here are some ways in which boundary establishment strengthens your self-trust:

Affirmation of Authenticity: When you set boundaries, you are essentially affirming your authenticity and individuality. You are communicating to the world who you are and what matters to you. This clarity and authenticity breed a sense of confidence, because you are being true to yourself and others.

Practice of Self-Care: Setting boundaries is a tangible form of self-care. You are prioritizing your own needs and well-being, demonstrating that you deserve to be treated with respect. The act of self-care, even if it means saying no to others, contributes to a healthy self-esteem and a sense of deserving.

Exercise of Self-Empowerment: By establishing boundaries, you are exercising your personal power. You are acknowledging that you have the right and authority to create boundaries that safeguard your peace, energy, and values. This exercise of self-empowerment nurtures your confidence, as you are acting as an active advocate for your own needs.

Recognition of Your Worth: Setting boundaries sends a powerful message to yourself and others: you value yourself. When you value yourself enough not to allow others to disrespect you or invade your privacy, you are internally reinforcing the idea that you deserve to be treated with dignity and consideration.

Development of Assertiveness: Boundary-setting involves the practice of assertiveness, which is the ability to express your needs and opinions respectfully and clearly. The more you engage in this process, the more you enhance your communication and assertiveness skills. This not only fortifies your confidence but also makes you more adept at facing challenging situations.

Creation of Positive Experiences: When you set boundaries and advocate for your needs, you create more positive experiences for yourself. This can include healthy relationships, reduced stress and anxiety, and a greater sense of balance. These positive experiences contribute to the cultivation of confidence, as you witness the positive outcomes of acting in favor of your well-being.

Cycle of Positive Reinforcement: Successful boundary establishment creates a cycle of positive reinforcement. The more you realize your self-trust is growing, the more motivated you become to continue practicing healthy boundaries. This cycle of reinforcement further bolsters your belief in your own abilities and value.

The fortification of self-trust is one of the most significant benefits of setting healthy boundaries. By asserting your authenticity, practicing self-care, exercising self-empowerment, and recognizing your intrinsic worth, you are building a strong foundation for a positive self-image and enduring self-confidence. As you engage in boundary definition, you are, in essence, nurturing your self-confidence and reaffirming your capacity to make decisions that promote your well-being and honor who you are.

Avoidance of Overwhelm and Resentment

Establishing healthy boundaries is not just an act of emotional self-preservation, but also plays a pivotal role in preventing overwhelm and the buildup of resentment. When you set clear boundaries and assertively communicate your needs, you are effectively safeguarding your energy and well-being. Here are some of the ways in which boundary setting helps to avoid overwhelm and resentment:

Energy Preservation: Setting boundaries is like forging a protective shield that preserves your energy. You establish reasonable amounts of time and resources for activities and commitments that hold the greatest significance for you. By avoiding the deluge of excessive obligations, you have more energy to invest in the areas that truly matter, which can help to alleviate the feeling of perpetual exhaustion.

Focus on Priorities: By setting boundaries, you are prioritizing your own needs and goals. This helps to direct your attention to what is truly essential, rather than spreading your efforts in multiple directions. This can help to ward off mental overwhelm that can come from trying to juggle too much at once, and can help you stay focused on your true objectives.

Prevention of Commitment Overload: In the absence of clearly defined boundaries, there is a tendency to take on an excessive number of commitments, often out of a fear of disappointing others. This can lead to a surplus of tasks and responsibilities that can undermine your quality of life. By setting boundaries, you can avoid the trap of overcommitment and make decisions that are more aligned with your priorities.

Mitigation of Stress and Anxiety: Overwhelm that stems from a lack of boundaries can lead to elevated levels of stress and anxiety. The constant pressure to fulfill obligations and demands can take a toll on your mental and emotional well-being. By establishing clear boundaries, you can reduce this pressure, which can create space for self-care and tranquility.

Maintenance of Equilibrium: Setting boundaries can help to maintain a healthy equilibrium among work, personal life, and relationships. By avoiding overindulgence in any one area, you can tend to all the important aspects of your existence. This can help to prevent any one area from consuming an excessive share of your energy, which can help to uphold an equilibrium that is conducive to overall well-being.

Prevention of Resentment: Consistently overstepping your own boundaries to cater to the demands of others can put you at risk of harboring resentment. Resentment can grow when you feel unjustly treated or undervalued due to constantly acquiescing to the needs of others. By setting boundaries and asserting your needs, you can preempt the buildup of resentment that can undermine relationships and emotional health.

Creation of Space for Self-Care: Boundary setting can create space for self-care. By avoiding the deluge of commitments and responsibilities, you can cultivate more time and energy to devote to activities that rejuvenate your spirit, such as indulging in hobbies, meditation, or simply unwinding. This can contribute to heightened emotional equilibrium and mitigate the risk of burnout.

Setting healthy boundaries is an effective strategy for avoiding overwhelm and resentment in your life. By preserving your energy, honing in on your priorities, avoiding commitment overload, and nurturing equilibrium, you are bolstering your emotional and mental well-being. Additionally, you are safeguarding your self-esteem by ensuring that your needs and values are honored. The result is a more balanced, rewarding life that is more aligned with your personal goals.

Enhancement of Relationships

Establishing healthy boundaries not only bolsters your self-esteem and well-being, but also has a significant impact on the enhancement of interpersonal relationships. When you communicate clearly and assertively about your needs and expectations, you cultivate an environment of mutual respect and understanding. Here are some of the ways in which establishing healthy boundaries can amplify your relationships:

Transparent Communication: By delineating boundaries, you are fostering transparent and open communication. This helps to avoid misunderstandings and confusion that can arise when expectations are unclear. Expressing your needs and limits forthrightly creates a space for candid dialogue and a solid foundation for the relationship.

Mutual Respect: Setting boundaries is an act of self-respect, while also exemplifying respect for others. By articulating your boundaries, you provide others with a clear understanding of how you wish to be treated. This engenders an atmosphere of mutual respect, where both parties feel valued and heard.

Prevention of Unnecessary Conflicts: Many conflicts in relationships stem from unmet expectations and overstepped boundaries. By setting boundaries from the outset and communicating them clearly, you can diminish the likelihood of unnecessary conflicts. This establishes a more harmonious environment where differences can be avoided or constructively resolved.

Trust Building: When you define and uphold your boundaries, you are building trust with others. They know they can rely on your honesty regarding your needs and expectations, which forms a solid bedrock of trust. This encourages others to feel at ease in sharing their own needs and concerns.

Fostering Authentic Relationships: Establishing healthy boundaries fosters authentic relationships. When you communicate honestly and assertively, you enable others to truly know you. This helps to build deeper, more meaningful connections where both parties can be genuine and vulnerable without fear of judgment.

Respect for Individual Differences: Boundary-setting also acknowledges and respects individual differences. Each person has their own needs, values, and boundaries, and by setting boundaries, you are demonstrating acceptance and understanding of these differences. This creates an inclusive environment where everyone feels valued for who they are.

Harmony Promotion: Relationships built upon healthy boundaries tend to be more harmonious. Involved parties understand their responsibilities and expectations, which minimizes the potential for misunderstandings. This cultivates a tranquil and collaborative atmosphere where all can focus on enjoying their time together.

Cultivation of Collective Growth: Setting healthy boundaries enables collective growth. When boundaries are respected, each person has space to flourish individually, and concurrently, the relationship as a whole thrives. This fosters a positive dynamic where both parties support each other's goals and aspirations.

Establishing healthy boundaries is not just a matter of self-esteem, it also has a significant impact on interpersonal relationships. The clear communication of needs and expectations engenders an environment of respect, trust, and harmony. This drives the construction of authentic and meaningful relationships, wherein both parties can grow and evolve together. Remember that setting boundaries is not merely about self-protection, it is also about forging stronger and healthier connections with others.

STRATEGIES FOR ASSERTIVELY COMMUNICATING YOUR NEEDS

Assertive communication is an art that enables you to express your needs and desires clearly and respectfully, without being aggressive or passive. Here are some strategies for communicating your needs assertively:

Familiarize Yourself with Your Needs and Boundaries

Before embarking on any conversation about setting boundaries and communicating your needs, it is paramount that you have a deep understanding of your own needs and boundaries. This self-awareness is the foundation of assertive and effective communication. Here are some ways to get acquainted with your needs and boundaries:

Explore Your Needs: To define boundaries and communicate your needs, it is essential to first identify what you require. This involves an introspective exploration of your emotions, desires, values, and priorities. Set aside time to connect with your feelings and understand what truly matters to you in a relationship, whether it be emotional, physical, mental, or spiritual.

Reflect on Your Boundaries: In addition to recognizing your needs, it is equally important to establish your boundaries. This means understanding how far you are willing to go in terms of commitments, time availability, levels of intimacy, and tolerance for certain behaviors. Ask yourself what you find acceptable and what would violate your personal limits.

Self-Knowledge and Self-Esteem: The process of understanding your needs and boundaries is closely linked to self-love. The more you know yourself, the more you demonstrate the respect you hold for yourself. This strengthens your self-esteem, enabling you to enter relationships with confidence and assertiveness. When you are aware of what you deserve and require, you are in a position to communicate it to others in a respectful manner.

Explore Past Experiences: Delving into your past experiences can also help you identify your needs and boundaries. Reflect on past relationships and situations that made you feel uncomfortable, unhappy, or disrespected. This can provide valuable insights into the types of situations or behaviors you wish to avoid or address differently in the future.

The Importance of Self-Empathy: As you explore your needs and boundaries, it is important to practice self-empathy. This means treating yourself with kindness and understanding, rather than judging or criticizing yourself for your choices and feelings. Recognize that your needs are valid and deserve to be met. Self-empathy can help you communicate your needs calmly and respectfully.

Regular Reflection Practice: Self-awareness and understanding your needs and boundaries are ongoing processes. As you grow and evolve, your needs may change. Therefore, it is important to set aside regular intervals for self-assessment, reflecting on your relationships, and adjusting your boundaries as needed.

Familiarity with your needs and boundaries not only provides you with a solid foundation for assertive communication, but it also fosters a healthier relationship with yourself. This is essential for setting effective boundaries and communicating your needs clearly and respectfully to others. By engaging in this process of self-exploration, you empower yourself to create relationships that are more genuine and fulfilling.

Selecting the Opportune Moment

Choosing the right time to communicate your needs is a critical aspect of assertive communication. This not only affects how your messages are received, but it can also determine the success of the conversation.

Taking into Account Emotions and Circumstances: One of the most important factors to consider when choosing the right time to address your needs is to think about both your emotions and the emotions of the other person. Avoid bringing up sensitive or important topics when either you or the other person is emotionally charged, stressed, or angry. During such times, the likelihood of constructive communication is diminished, and the conversation can easily turn into conflict.

Seeking an Appropriate Environment: It is also essential to find a conducive environment for the conversation. A calm and private setting where both of you can focus on the conversation is better suited for discussing important needs. Avoid distractions or interruptions that could diminish the quality of the conversation. If possible, choose a time when both of you are relaxed and have the time to engage in the discussion.

Avoiding Public Confrontations: Avoid discussing delicate or personal matters in public or in front of others.

This can cause embarrassment and increase emotional stress, making it difficult for both parties to express themselves honestly and empathetically.

Noting Readiness Cues: Sometimes, it can be helpful to look for cues that the other person is ready to have a serious conversation. If the person seems open, relaxed, and willing to communicate, it can be a sign that the timing is right. Conversely, if the person is preoccupied, distracted, or seems tense, it is advisable to postpone the discussion until a more opportune time.

Preplanning: Planning the conversation in advance can also help you identify the right moment. You could even let the other person know that you want to discuss something important and ask when would be a good time for them. This shows consideration for their time and emotional state, creating a more receptive environment for communication.

Keeping the Conversation's Purpose in Mind: It is important to keep the conversation's purpose in mind when choosing the right moment. Think about why you are communicating these needs and what you hope to achieve through the conversation. This can help you assess whether the current moment is right or if it would be better to wait for a more opportune time.

Choosing the right moment to communicate your needs shows your respect for the emotional well-being of both parties. This increases the likelihood that the conversation will be well-received and conducted in a constructive manner. Remember that assertive communication is not just about what you say, but also about the context in which you choose to express your needs.

Employing Clear and Direct Language

The way you articulate your needs plays a pivotal role in the effectiveness of assertive communication. Using clear and direct language is essential to ensuring that your messages are understood without ambiguity.

Avoiding Ambiguity: It is crucial to avoid ambiguity in communication. Use words and phrases that are unambiguous and unequivocal. Avoid overly complex language, jargon, or vague expressions that could lead to misinterpretation. The clearer your language, the less room there is for misunderstandings.

Being Objective and Concise: Communicate in an objective and concise manner. Get to the point without using too many words. This not only helps with comprehension, but it also keeps the focus on the core message. Use short and straightforward sentences to effectively convey your needs.

Using Concrete Examples: When conveying your needs, use concrete examples to illustrate your point. This makes communication more tangible and helps the other person understand the situation better. Examples can also help to avoid misconceptions, as concrete situations are easier to understand.

Avoiding Vagueness and Generalizations: Avoid vague terms or generalizations that could create confusion. Instead of saying something like, "I sometimes feel like you don't understand me," be more specific, such as, "When we discuss my work, I feel like you're not addressing my concerns."

Ensuring Comprehension: After communicating your needs, it is wise to ensure that the other person understands you correctly. You can do this by asking, "Does this make sense to you?" or "Do you understand what I'm trying to say?" This gives the other person the opportunity to clarify any points that may not be clear.

Avoiding Aggressive Language: While clarity is important, it is equally important to avoid aggressive or domineering language. Remember that the goal of assertive communication is to express your needs in a respectful and constructive manner. Aggressive language can elicit defensiveness in the other person and compromise the quality of the conversation.

Reviewing and Refining: Throughout the communication process, you can quickly review your words to ensure that your language is clear and direct. Sometimes, rephrasing a sentence or choosing different words can make your message more comprehensible.

Exhibiting Patience: If the other person struggles to understand your message, be patient. Present it in a different way or use alternative examples to ensure that your needs are adequately communicated. Clear communication requires empathy and a willingness to ensure that all parties are on the same page.

Using clear and direct language is an effective way to ensure that your needs are understood precisely. This helps to prevent misunderstandings and contributes to successful assertive communication.

Maintain a Focus on Yourself

A fundamental approach to assertively communicating your needs is to maintain a focus on yourself. This means expressing your emotions, thoughts, and desires without blaming or accusing others. By doing so, you create an environment of more open communication where the other person is more likely to listen and understand your needs. Here are some ways to maintain a focus on yourself during communication:

Avoid Blame and Accusations: When you blame or accuse someone, it is more likely that they will become defensive. This can lead to an unproductive conversation where both parties are more focused on defending themselves than on resolving the issue. By keeping the focus on yourself, you can avoid the cycle of blame and accusations and allow the conversation to flow more constructively.

Express Your Feelings and Needs: Instead of saying something like "You always get this wrong," you can say "I feel frustrated when things don't go according to plan." Sharing your personal feelings and needs helps the other person understand how their actions or words impact you. This creates a more empathetic foundation for the conversation.

Foster Empathy and Understanding: When you share your feelings and needs, you are inviting the other person to see things from your perspective. This fosters empathy and understanding as the other person begins to see situations from your point of view. This can lead to a more collaborative discussion and the pursuit of mutually satisfactory solutions.

Be Transparent and Authentic: Focusing on yourself allows you to be authentic and transparent in communication. You are expressing your genuine experience, which builds trust in the conversation. Emotional honesty is an essential part of assertive communication, and keeping the focus on yourself helps to nurture it.

Avoid Judgments and Criticisms: By keeping the focus on yourself, you avoid making judgments or criticisms about the other person. This creates a space where both parties can feel more comfortable sharing openly without fear of being evaluated or criticized. Communication becomes more focused on problem-solving and understanding perspectives.

Use "I" Statements: A practical strategy for maintaining a focus on yourself is to use "I" statements. This helps to underscore that you are sharing your own experiences and perceptions, rather than attributing responsibility to others. "I" statements are also less threatening and more likely to be well-received.

Emphasize Collaboration: When the focus is on yourself, you are inviting the other person to join you in seeking a solution. This fosters a sense of collaboration where both parties work together to resolve an issue or meet a need. Communication becomes more constructive and results-oriented.

By maintaining a focus on yourself during communication, you are creating an environment where your needs can be understood and addressed more effectively. This establishes a solid foundation for conflict resolution, joint decision-making, and the cultivation of healthier relationships.

Using the First-Person Perspective Instead of "You"

The way we choose our words in conversation can have a big impact on how the message is received. One incredibly effective way to assertively express your needs is to use statements that start with "I" instead of "you." This approach puts the focus on your own emotions and experiences, rather than pointing fingers at the other person. Here are some of the benefits of using "I" instead of "you" in communication:

Avoiding Attacks and Blame: When we use statements that start with "you," it can sound like we are accusing or blaming the other person. This can lead to immediate defensiveness and a tense conversation. For example, saying "You never help me around the house" can come across as an attack. By using "I," the emphasis shifts to how you feel and what you need, making communication less threatening.

Expressing Personal Emotions: Using "I" allows you to express your own personal emotions more directly. For example, saying "I feel hurt when we don't spend time together" communicates how you are feeling and opens the door to a more empathetic conversation. Personal emotions are hard to dispute, as they are your genuine experiences.

Focusing on Individual Perception: Statements that start with "I" underscore that you are sharing your individual perception of the situation. This prevents the other person from feeling judged or criticized. By communicating how you perceive things, you invite the other person to understand your viewpoint instead of feeling attacked.

Promoting Mutual Understanding: By using "I," you are conveying your own needs and perspectives, establishing an environment of more open dialogue. This fosters mutual understanding, as the other person is more inclined to listen and respond constructively. Communication becomes less defensive and more focused on problem-solving.

Creating Space for Collaboration: Statements that start with "I" are less confrontational and more likely to create space for collaboration. By expressing your needs on a personal level, you are inviting the other person to join you in the pursuit of a solution. This can lead to more productive conversations and the search for common ground.

Being Authentic and Transparent: Using "I" instead of "you" is a way of being authentic and transparent in communication. You are sharing your own experiences and feelings, which establishes an environment of trust and honesty. This allows the other person to perceive your sincerity and paves the way for a more genuine discussion.

By embracing the strategy of using "I" instead of "you" during communication, you are building a solid foundation for assertively expressing your needs and emotions. This approach promotes more respectful, empathetic, and constructive dialogue, contributing to healthy relationships and effective communication.

Exude Steadfastness with Respect

When it comes to assertively communicating your needs, it is important to strike a balance between steadfastness and respect. Being firm does not mean being aggressive, and being respectful does not mean being passive. Here are some tips on how to adopt an approach that embodies both resolute determination and respect when articulating your needs:

Establish Boundaries with Steadfastness: This means communicating your needs in a clear and unflinching manner. You are setting a healthy boundary for what is acceptable and what is not. However, it is important to remember that being firm does not mean being inflexible. You can assert your position without being rigid.

Maintain a Calm Tone of Voice: A composed and controlled tone of voice is essential when communicating your needs respectfully. Avoid raising your voice or resorting to aggressive language. A calm tone will help keep the conversation at an emotionally appropriate level and create an environment conducive to understanding.

Avoid Confrontations and Personal Attacks: While being firm, it is important to avoid falling into the trap of becoming confrontational. Focus on the issues and needs at hand, rather than attacking the other person personally. Personal criticism and attacks can lead to defensiveness and negative communication. Instead, focus on the other person's actions or behavior, not on their character.

Convey Conviction with Respect: Demonstrating firmness means expressing your conviction and confidence in your needs without belittling the perspective of the other person. Demonstrate that you take your own needs and expectations seriously, but are also willing to listen and understand the other person's viewpoint.

Exemplify Openness to Dialogue: Being firm does not mean shutting the door to dialogue. Be open to hearing what the other person has to say and to finding mutual solutions. Firmness should not preclude the possibility of finding common ground or reaching an agreement that meets the needs of both parties.

Practice Empathy: In conjunction with firmness, it is also important to practice empathy. Put yourself in the other person's shoes and try to understand their concerns or perspectives. Empathy will foster more compassionate and respectful communication, even when you are steadfastly advocating for your needs.

Respect Divergent Opinions: Not everyone will always agree with your needs or boundaries. Being firm in such situations means maintaining your position respectfully, even in the face of differing opinions. Be willing to calmly explain your reasoning and listen to others' viewpoints while upholding mutual respect.

Champion Constructive Resolution: An approach that intertwines firmness and respect in communicating your needs will contribute to constructive conflict resolution. You are demonstrating your commitment to your needs while being open to collaborating to find solutions that benefit both parties. This will foster collaboration and understanding.

By harmonizing steadfastness with respect, you are building a foundation for effective communication and advocating for your needs in a healthy manner. This will lead to more harmonious relationships and facilitate the constructive resolution of conflicts.

Embrace the Possibility of Negotiation

When it comes to assertively communicating your needs, being open to negotiation is a fundamental attitude. Effective communication is not just about expressing your own needs, but also about listening to the other person's perspective and working collaboratively to find solutions that meet both parties' needs. The importance of being open to negotiation:

The Power of Bidirectional Communication: Communication is not a unilateral process; it is an exchange between two individuals. Being willing to listen to the other person's viewpoints is essential for a healthy dialogue. Negotiation involves sharing perspectives, interests, and concerns from both sides to find common ground.

Respect for Both Parties' Needs: By being open to negotiation, you demonstrate respect for the other person's needs and perspectives. This creates an environment where both parties feel valued and heard. Negotiation is not about one side winning and the other losing, but about finding a balance that works for both.

Exploration of Creative Solutions: Negotiation is not just about conceding or compromising; it can also be an opportunity to explore creative solutions that meet both parties' needs in innovative ways. By opening up to different possibilities, you may come up with solutions that were not originally considered.

Avoidance of Rigidity: Being open to negotiation helps avoid rigid or inflexible positions. This allows you to adjust your own expectations and needs based on feedback from the other party. Negotiation fosters an attitude of flexibility and adaptability, which is essential for healthy relationships.

Building Mutual Understanding: Effective negotiation builds mutual understanding. By carefully considering the other person's concerns and perspectives, you are laying the foundation for deeper, more meaningful communication. This contributes to a more harmonious relationship and the constructive resolution of conflicts.

Overcoming Deadlocks: In some cases, negotiations may lead to deadlocks or disagreements. However, being open to negotiation also means being willing to explore ways to overcome these impasses. This may sometimes require additional time to consider different options or find compromises that benefit both parties.

Staying Focused on Solutions: During negotiation, it is important to stay focused on solutions and underlying needs. Avoid clinging to rigid positions or engaging in unproductive disputes. Focus on devising ways to meet the needs of both parties and moving forward constructively.

Learning and Growth: Being open to negotiation provides an opportunity for learning and growth. You can gain valuable insights about the other person and how to collaborate effectively. This approach also allows you to refine your communication and conflict resolution skills.

By embracing the possibility of negotiation, you are building a relationship based on mutual understanding, collaboration, and respect. This approach contributes to healthier communication and the development of solutions that meet the needs of both sides.

Embrace the Possibility of Negotiation

When it comes to assertively communicating your needs, being open to negotiation is a fundamental attitude. Effective communication is not just about expressing your own needs, but also about listening to the other person's perspective and working collaboratively to find solutions that meet both parties' needs. The importance of being open to negotiation:

The Power of Bidirectional Communication: Communication is not a unilateral process; it is an exchange between two individuals. Being willing to listen to the other person's viewpoints is essential for a healthy dialogue. Negotiation involves sharing perspectives, interests, and concerns from both sides to find common ground.

Respect for Both Parties' Needs: By being open to negotiation, you demonstrate respect for the other person's needs and perspectives. This creates an environment where both parties feel valued and heard. Negotiation is not about one side winning and the other losing, but about finding a balance that works for both.

Exploration of Creative Solutions: Negotiation is not just about conceding or compromising; it can also be an opportunity to explore creative solutions that meet both parties' needs in innovative ways. By opening up to different possibilities, you may come up with solutions that were not originally considered.

Avoidance of Rigidity: Being open to negotiation helps avoid rigid or inflexible positions. This allows you to adjust your own expectations and needs based on feedback from the other party. Negotiation fosters an attitude of flexibility and adaptability, which is essential for healthy relationships.

Building Mutual Understanding: Effective negotiation builds mutual understanding. By carefully considering the other person's concerns and perspectives, you are laying the foundation for deeper, more meaningful communication. This contributes to a more harmonious relationship and the constructive resolution of conflicts.

Overcoming Deadlocks: In some cases, negotiations may lead to deadlocks or disagreements. However, being open to negotiation also means being willing to explore ways to overcome these impasses. This may sometimes require additional time to consider different options or find compromises that benefit both parties.

Staying Focused on Solutions: During negotiation, it is important to stay focused on solutions and underlying needs. Avoid clinging to rigid positions or engaging in unproductive disputes. Focus on devising ways to meet the needs of both parties and moving forward constructively.

Learning and Growth: Being open to negotiation provides an opportunity for learning and growth. You can gain valuable insights about the other person and how to collaborate effectively. This approach also allows you to refine your communication and conflict resolution skills.

By embracing the possibility of negotiation, you are building a relationship based on mutual understanding, collaboration, and respect. This approach contributes to healthier communication and the development of solutions that meet the needs of both sides.

Embrace Empathy

Empathy is an essential skill in the realm of assertive communication. It involves the ability to put oneself in the shoes of another person, to understand their feelings and perspectives, and to respond with sensitivity and compassion. Through the practice of empathy during communication, you create an environment of mutual understanding and respect. The significance of practicing empathy while expressing your needs:

Forging Meaningful Connections: Empathy is a powerful way to foster meaningful connections with others. By striving to understand the emotions and viewpoints of the other person, you show genuine concern for their well-being. This strengthens the foundation of relationships and promotes more positive communication.

Fostering Openness: Through empathy, you encourage the other person to feel comfortable sharing their feelings and perspectives. When people feel heard and understood, they are more likely to express themselves openly. This contributes to communication that is more honest and transparent.

Averting Misunderstandings: Empathy can help to avoid misunderstandings and misconstrued interpretations. By putting yourself in the other person's shoes, you are better able to discern whether your words or actions might be construed differently from your intentions. This mitigates the risk of conflict and misinterpretations.

Respecting Divergent Perspectives: Everyone brings their own experiences, values, and beliefs that shape their worldview. Practicing empathy means acknowledging and respecting these differences. While you might not necessarily agree with the other person, you can still respect their perspective and seek common ground.

Cultivating Trust: Empathy contributes to the cultivation of trust. When people sense that you care about their feelings and viewpoints, they are more likely to trust you. This is particularly important when communicating needs, as trust facilitates a positive and open response.

Diminishing Defensiveness: The practice of empathy can help to diminish defensiveness during challenging conversations. When you demonstrate awareness of the other person's emotions, they are less likely to feel attacked or judged. This fosters a more constructive and less reactive dialogue.

Creating an Environment of Mutual Respect: Empathy engenders an environment of mutual respect, where both parties feel valued and heard. This paves the way for openness in sharing needs and concerns candidly. As each person feels understood, communication becomes more productive.

Encouraging Cooperation and Collaboration: Empathy incentivizes cooperation and collaboration. By showing a willingness to understand the other person's feelings, they are more likely to engage in joint efforts to find solutions. This is particularly advantageous when dealing with complex or contentious situations.

Facilitating Profound Understanding: Through practicing empathy, you seek a profound understanding of the other person's emotions and concerns. This enables you to communicate more effectively, addressing underlying issues and responding to genuine needs.

Practicing empathy during communication not only strengthens relationships, but it also fosters an atmosphere of understanding, respect, and cooperation. Empathy is a powerful tool for connecting with others meaningfully and creating a climate of healthy communication.

Embrace Consistency

Establishing boundaries and assertively communicating your needs is not a one-time event, but rather an ongoing practice that demands steadfast consistency over time. This unwavering dedication is paramount for nurturing healthy relationships, as well as safeguarding your self-esteem and emotional well-being. The significance of consistency in setting boundaries:

Demonstration of Integrity: Staying consistent with your limits and needs shows your integrity. When you uphold your word and adhere to the boundaries you have set, others perceive you as a reliable and respectable individual. This bolsters trust in your interactions.

Creation of Clear Expectations: Consistency leads to clear expectations for others. When people recognize that you consistently act in alignment with your values and boundaries, they are more likely to respect those boundaries. This also mitigates ambiguity and misunderstandings.

Respect for Your Emotional Well-Being: By staying consistent in upholding your boundaries, you are prioritizing your emotional well-being. This prevents you from becoming overwhelmed by excessive commitments or situations that are misaligned with your values. Consistency is an act of self-care.

Prevention of Confusion and Conflict: A lack of consistency can lead to confusion and conflict. If you set boundaries at one moment and then allow them to be violated at another, this can create uncertainty and resentment. Consistency prevents misunderstandings and helps maintain harmony in relationships.

Fortification of Self-Esteem: Consistency fortifies your self-esteem. When you steadfastly advocate for your needs and values, you are sending a message to yourself that you hold your worth and deserve respect. This contributes to a positive self-image.

Sustaining Mutual Respect: Consistency helps uphold mutual respect in relationships. When others perceive that you are consistent in upholding your boundaries, they are more likely to respect those boundaries as well.

This creates an environment where everyone is treated with consideration.

Encouragement of Healthy Relationships: Consistency is a key ingredient for healthy relationships. Relationships grounded in mutual respect and trust are often built upon the foundation of consistency. This enables individuals to feel secure and valued within the relationship.

Fostering Personal Growth: The consistent practice of setting boundaries and assertively communicating needs also fosters personal growth. As you strive to maintain consistency, you are developing skills in communication, self-awareness, and self-discipline. This contributes to your own development.

Reflecting Your Commitment to Healthy Relationships: Consistency reflects your commitment to healthy and respectful relationships. By steadfastly upholding your boundaries and needs, you send the message that you value the quality of your interactions and are willing to act in alignment with those values.

Ultimately, consistency in setting boundaries and assertively communicating needs not only fortifies relationships, but also bolsters your self-esteem, fosters mutual understanding, and contributes to a wholesome and respectful environment. By being consistent, you are investing in your own well-being and the quality of your relationships.

Embrace the Fearless "No"

Speaking the word "no" is an essential skill in the realm of assertive communication and setting healthy boundaries. While it can be daunting, it's important to remember that saying "no" when necessary is not rude, selfish, or negative. In fact, it can be a powerful way to protect your emotional well-being, set clear boundaries, and prioritize your personal needs. Here are some reasons why you shouldn't be afraid to say "no":

Self-Empowerment: Saying "no" is an act of self-empowerment. When you express your unwillingness to participate in activities that are not aligned with your values, you are taking control of your life and your choices. This can help to boost your self-esteem and sense of autonomy.

Boundary Setting: Saying "no" is a way to set boundaries and assert your needs. When you give in to requests that don't feel right for you, you are essentially giving others permission to cross your boundaries. Saying "no" can help you to uphold your boundaries and communicate that you are willing to take care of yourself.

Emotional Health: Prioritizing your emotional health is essential, and saying "no" when necessary can be a key part of that process. When you are feeling overwhelmed by commitments, stress, or emotional exhaustion, saying "no" can help to protect your mental and emotional well-being.

Self-Respect: Saying "no" is an act of self-respect. When you decline requests that are not in alignment with your values, you are communicating that you value yourself and your time. This can send a powerful message to others about how you expect to be treated.

Clear Communication: A direct and respectful "no" can be a beacon of clear communication. It can help to avoid misunderstandings and misinterpretations. When you are honest about your limitations and availability, others in your life will have a clear understanding of your boundaries.

Ensuring Alignment with Values: Saying "no" can help you to ensure that your endeavors are aligned with your values and goals. This means focusing your energy on activities and relationships that are personally meaningful and rewarding.

Avoiding Resentment: Often, giving in to unwanted requests or situations can lead to resentment and disappointment. A respectful "no" can help you to avoid feeling overwhelmed or trapped in situations that are not conducive to your well-being.

Promoting Authentic Relationships: Selectively saying "no" to situations that warrant it can also promote authentic relationships. It allows you to be honest and transparent in your interactions. Others in your life will appreciate your honesty and may be more likely to embrace authenticity themselves.

Creating a Culture of Mutual Respect: By saying "no" in an assertive and respectful way, you can lay the foundation for a culture of healthy and respectful communication. This can create an environment where those around you are more likely to acknowledge and respect your boundaries, leading to more harmonious relationships.

Encouraging Self-Care: Saying "no" when necessary is an act of self-care. It emphasizes your willingness to prioritize your needs and take care of yourself. This is an essential part of maintaining a balance between your obligations and your personal well-being.

Defining limits and saying "no" are essential components of a balanced and healthy life. When you put your own needs first and assert your boundaries in an assertive way, you protect your emotional, mental, and physical well-being. Remember that saying "no" is an act of self-love and self-respect. By mastering these skills, you can create an environment where your needs are met, your relationships are more respectful, and you can live an authentic and meaningful life.

CHAPTER 8

NOURISHING SELF-LOVE IN DAILY LIFE

**Self-love flourishes
with each choice that honors
the essence of who you are.**

Nurturing self-love is an ongoing commitment that demands daily practice and unwavering attention. The journey of crafting a wholesome relationship with oneself is laden with self-discovery, introspection, and self-care. In this chapter, we shall delve deeper, uncovering ways to seamlessly integrate this lifelong practice into your daily routine, embracing minuscule habits that elevate your self-esteem and well-being.

SUBTLE HABITS ENRICHING YOUR SELF-CONNECTION

The tapestry of our self-connection is woven through everyday interactions, and weaving in subtle habits can profoundly fortify this bond:

Daily Self-Acceptance

Self-acceptance is an act of profound self-love. Initiating each morning with a commitment to embrace oneself exactly as is, is a powerful practice that nurtures one's self-relationship. Here are some contemplations on how to foster daily self-acceptance:

Cultivating Self-Compassion: Self-compassion involves treating oneself with the same kindness and understanding that would be extended to a cherished friend. When self-critical thoughts arise, remember to be gentle with yourself, as you would with someone you hold dear.

Embracing Qualities and Imperfections: Self-acceptance encompasses embracing all facets of oneself, both the qualities you hold in high esteem and the imperfections you acknowledge. Recognize that being human is synonymous with being imperfect, and that your flaws are integral to your journey.

Challenging Limiting Beliefs: Identify and challenge limiting beliefs that lead you to self-criticism. Often, these beliefs are internalized from past experiences. Questioning these beliefs aids in constructing a healthier self-image.

Cultivating Self-Confidence: Self-acceptance is intimately intertwined with self-confidence. By acknowledging and valuing your skills and accomplishments, you lay a sturdy foundation for trusting in yourself and approaching challenges positively.

Fostering Positive Inner Dialogue: Observe how you speak to yourself internally. Transform the critical voice into one that is encouraging and supportive. Replace self-criticisms with affirmative statements.

Allowing the Growth Process: Acknowledge that personal growth involves learning from mistakes and evolving through experiences. Self-acceptance does not equate to complacency, but rather allowing oneself to evolve healthily.

Grasping Shared Humanity: Understand that everyone carries their internal struggles and challenges.

Realizing that you are not alone in your experiences can help cultivate self-empathy.

Exercising Patience: Self-acceptance is a continuous process. Be patient with yourself as you work toward nurturing a more loving and positive self-relationship. Progress unfolds gradually.

Cultivating Emotional Resilience: By accepting your emotions and permitting yourself to feel, you foster emotional resilience. Embrace the notion that feelings of vulnerability are also part of your humanity.

Daily self-acceptance is an investment in your emotional and mental well-being. Keep in mind that you are deserving of love and respect, exactly as you are. As you internalize this truth, you fortify your foundation of self-love and construct a positive and resilient self-image.

Empowering Affirmations

Positive affirmations are valuable tools for reprogramming your mind and nurturing self-love. By incorporating affirmative declarations into your daily routine, you take tangible steps towards transforming your self-relationship. Here are some tips on how to effectively utilize positive affirmations:

Identify Limiting Beliefs: Before selecting affirmations, pinpoint the self-critical beliefs you wish to challenge. These beliefs often manifest as negative self-talk. For example, if you tend to feel inadequate, an affirmation could be: "I am enough exactly as I am."

Craft Evidence-Based Affirmations: Craft affirmations grounded in real evidence of your past achievements and qualities. This makes the affirmations more compelling and helps to counter internal negativity.

Choose Realistic Affirmations: Choose affirmations that resonate with you and are realistic. Overly extravagant affirmations may be hard to believe. Be gentle with yourself and generate affirmations that are aligned with your aspirations and values.

Practice Regularly: Consistent practice is essential. Set aside a specific time each day to recite your affirmations. It could be in the morning, evening, or whenever you feel the need. The more you repeat them, the deeper these affirmations will embed in your mind.

Visualize the Positive: As you recite your affirmations, endeavor to visualize the positive reality they represent. Imagine yourself facing challenges with confidence, expressing self-love, and succeeding. This visualization strengthens the link between affirmations and positive feelings.

Use Present Tense Language: Phrase your affirmations in the present tense, as if they are already happening. This reinforces the notion that you are embodying these positive qualities in your life right now.

Connect with Your Emotions: While reciting your affirmations, strive to emotionally connect with them. Feel the positive impact of each affirmation on your self-esteem and self-confidence. This amplifies the potency of the practice.

Variety and Rotation: Over time, you can craft multiple affirmations for various areas of your life. This helps to address diverse self-critical beliefs and cultivate a more positive and comprehensive mindset.

Keep a Journal: Maintaining an affirmation journal can be beneficial. Jot down your daily affirmations and observe how your feelings and thoughts evolve towards yourself over time.

Be Persistent and Patient: Like any mindset shift, affirmations practice demands persistence and patience. Don't be discouraged if you don't immediately sense the effects. Over time, these affirmations will become a natural part of your mindset.

Adapt to Change: As you grow and evolve, your affirmations may change. Be open to adjusting your affirmations to reflect your progress and new goals.

Integrate into Daily Activities: In addition to setting aside dedicated time for reciting affirmations, you can also weave them into your daily routine. Utter your affirmations while showering, exercising, or performing household tasks.

Consistent practice of positive affirmations engenders a gradual shift in your mindset. With time, you will begin to discern a meaningful difference in how you perceive yourself and relate to your own being.

Commending Your Triumphs

Celebrating your triumphs is a tangible way to nurture self-love and forge a positive relationship with yourself. It goes beyond mere recognition; it fortifies your self-assurance, ignites motivation, and establishes a positive cycle of achievements. Here are some tips on how to maximize the art of celebrating your conquests:

Celebrate Progress, Not Just End Results: Don't limit your celebrations to grand achievements. Acknowledge the progress you make along the way. Each completed step, each surmounted hurdle, deserves celebration.

Set Success Milestones: Set specific and measurable goals for yourself. When you reach these milestones, give yourself a celebration. This will help you stay motivated and on track.

Acknowledge Small Victories: Sometimes, it's the small victories in everyday life that are the most meaningful. Take note of moments when you face a fear, meet a deadline, or triumph over a challenge. Each minor victory is a step towards greater self-esteem.

Celebrate Consistency: Consistency is a valuable virtue. Be proud of your ability to stick with your goals and see things through. This will help you build a strong foundation of self-confidence.

Keep an Archive of Your Triumphs: Keeping a journal of your accomplishments is a great way to track your progress. Record all of your achievements, big and small.

When you're feeling down, you can look back at your journal and remember how much you've accomplished.

Celebrate in a Way that Feels Meaningful to You: There's no right or wrong way to celebrate your triumphs. Find something that you enjoy and that makes you feel good. It could be anything from going out to dinner to taking a day trip to the spa.

Share Your Triumphs with Others: Sharing your successes with friends and family can be a great way to celebrate. They can join in on the festivities and help you reinforce the positive feelings associated with your achievements.

Cultivate Healthy Pride: It's important to be proud of your accomplishments, but it's also important to avoid arrogance. Healthy pride is about recognizing your efforts and merits without letting your ego get the best of you.

Accept Compliments Graciously: When others compliment you on your achievements, be sure to accept them graciously. Don't downplay your accomplishments or reject praise. This will help you internalize your capabilities and build your self-esteem.

Harness Celebration as Motivation: When you're facing new challenges, think back to your past celebrations. This can help you stay motivated and remind you that you've overcome obstacles before.

Celebrate Long-Term Achievements: In addition to celebrating your immediate successes, be sure to commemorate your long-term achievements as well. This could be a birthday, a graduation, or a professional milestone.

Reflect and Be Grateful: When you're celebrating, take some time to reflect on your journey. Think about the hard work you've put in, the lessons you've learned, and the people who have supported you along the way. Gratitude can amplify the positive feelings associated with your triumphs.

The consistent practice of celebrating your triumphs can create an emotionally buoyant environment within. This can boost your self-love, sense of self-appreciation, and motivation to pursue goals that fill you with pride and satisfaction.

The Practice of Gratitude

The practice of gratitude is a powerful tool that can transform your perspective and nurture self-love in your daily life. It is the art of focusing your attention on the things you are grateful for, which fosters an attitude of appreciation and positivity. Here are some additional ways to incorporate gratitude into your life:

Variety in Gratitude: Don't just focus on the big blessings in your life. Also be grateful for the small things, like the kindness of a stranger, a beautiful sunset, or even the things you often take for granted.

Gratitude Journal: Keep a journal where you write down three things you are grateful for each day. This exercise can help you focus on the positive aspects of your life and create a tangible record of your blessings.

Gratitude Visualization: Take a few minutes each day to close your eyes and visualize the things you are grateful for. Feel the joy and gratitude that these things bring you.

Create a Space of Gratitude: Designate a special place in your home for gratitude. This could be an altar, a vision board, or simply a corner where you keep items that symbolize your blessings.

Practice Gratitude for Challenges: In addition to being grateful for the positive things in your life, also be grateful for the challenges you face. Challenges can provide opportunities for growth and learning, even if they seem difficult in the moment.

Gratitude for Self-Care: Recognize and appreciate every act of self-care you take. This could include anything from taking a few minutes to meditate to making a healthy meal. Self-care is essential for your well-being.

Share Gratitude: Express your gratitude to others. This could be through a thank-you note, a text message, or even a simple gesture like holding the door open for someone. Sharing gratitude strengthens your relationships and creates a ripple effect of positivity.

Gratitude Meditation: Practice gratitude meditation, which involves focusing on the things you are thankful for. This can help to quiet your mind and increase your sense of well-being.

Gratitude for Authenticity: Be grateful for your authentic self. Embrace your unique qualities, your journey, and your experiences.

Gratitude for Self-Discovery: As you gain deeper self-awareness, express gratitude for the process of self-discovery. This includes acknowledging your strengths, weaknesses, and everything that makes you unique.

Gratitude for Transformation: As you mature and evolve, acknowledge the journey of transformation you are on. Be thankful for your capacity to adapt and learn.

Circle of Gratitude: Gather with friends or family on a regular basis to share what you are grateful for. This creates an atmosphere of positivity and encourages everyone to appreciate what they have.

The practice of gratitude can not only nurture self-love, but it can also boost mental well-being, increase emotional resilience, and contribute to a more positive outlook on life. The more you practice gratitude, the more consciously you will begin to perceive the many blessings in your life, which will help to create a virtuous cycle of self-love and appreciation.

Moments of Self-Reflection

Self-reflection is a practice that allows you to deepen your self-awareness, learn from past experiences, and foster personal growth. These moments of self-reflection are opportunities to forge a deeper connection with yourself and cultivate a richer understanding of your emotions, actions, and thoughts. Here are some ways to incorporate self-reflection into your daily routine:

Journaling: Keep a self-reflection journal where you chronicle your experiences, emotions, and insights throughout the day. Writing can help you process your feelings and identify patterns of behavior.

Empowering Questions: Ask yourself questions that encourage deep self-reflection. For example, "What did I learn today?", "How did I feel in different situations?", or "What could have been done differently?"

Identifying Challenges: Identify the challenges you encountered during the day. Reflect on how you navigated them and what you can learn from these situations.

Celebrating Achievements: Acknowledge your daily accomplishments, no matter how small. This can boost your self-esteem and encourage a positive self-attitude.

Analyzing Emotional Responses: Observe your emotional responses in different situations. Ask yourself why you felt a certain way and if there is a healthier way to address these emotions.

Recognizing Behavioral Patterns: Look for patterns in your behavior and reactions. This can help you understand your tendencies and make more conscious decisions in the future.

Identifying Instances of Self-Love: Identify the times when you practiced self-love throughout the day. This could involve setting boundaries, acknowledging your needs, or treating yourself with kindness.

Learning from Challenging Situations: Instead of viewing challenging situations negatively, view them as opportunities for learning. Ask yourself what you can take away from these experiences.

Setting Goals: Use self-reflection to set goals for the following day. Identify areas where you want to grow and how you can effectively practice self-love.

Cultivating Resilience: Reflect on how you faced adversity and challenges. This can help you build resilience and find ways to face difficulties in the future.

Valuing Lessons Learned: Recognize that each experience, even the difficult ones, can teach you something valuable. Gleaning insights from your experiences can contribute to your personal growth.

Practicing Forgiveness: Use self-reflection to practice self-forgiveness. Acknowledge times when you may have acted in ways that were not productive and allow yourself to learn and grow from them.

Making Decisions: When reflecting on your day's choices, evaluate how each decision aligned with your values and needs. This can help you make more informed decisions in the future.

The practice of self-reflection does not require a lot of time. It can be done before bed, during a quiet moment, or even during brief pauses throughout the day. The key is to cultivate the ability to look at yourself honestly and learn from your experiences. This will allow you to continuously grow on your journey of self-love.

These small habits can not only strengthen your relationship with yourself, but they can also create a positive and uplifting inner atmosphere. They are essential ingredients for nurturing self-love in your daily life and making it an integral part of your existence. By committing to these habits, you are investing in a lasting and fulfilling relationship with yourself.

CREATING A REGIMEN OF SELF-CARE AND PERSONAL VALUATION

Nurturing self-love in your daily life requires establishing a routine that prioritizes self-care and personal appreciation. These daily habits strengthen your connection with yourself and maintain a positive and enriching relationship:

Deliberate Dawns

Starting your day with an intentional morning regimen is a gift you give yourself. These initial moments of the day set the tone for how you will relate to yourself and the world in the hours that follow. Creating an intentional morning ritual is a powerful way to cultivate self-compassion and boost self-love. Here are some practices that can be woven into your mornings:

Morning Meditation: Set aside a few minutes for meditation early in the morning. Meditation helps calm the mind, nurture mindfulness, and forge a peaceful connection with yourself.

Gentle Stretching: Start your day with a few minutes of gentle stretching. This helps to awaken the body, improve circulation, and relieve any muscle tension from the night before.

Positive Affirmations: Recite positive affirmations as you prepare for the day. These affirmative statements can help you create a positive mindset and reinforce uplifting beliefs about yourself.

Inspirational Reading: Allocate time to read something inspirational or motivational. It could be an excerpt from a book, a poem, or a quote that resonates with you and boosts your positive mindset.

Journal Writing: Dedicate a few minutes to journal writing. You can chronicle your thoughts, feelings, daily goals, or anything else that's on your mind. This process can help you organize your thoughts and release emotions.

Positive Visualization: Engage in positive visualization of your day. Envision yourself facing the day's activities with confidence, completing tasks effortlessly, and addressing challenges with calm and centeredness.

Breakfast Time: Enjoy a nourishing and mindful breakfast. Eat with mindfulness, savoring each bite, and relishing the flavors and textures of the food.

Nature Connection: If possible, spend some time outdoors. Inhaling fresh air and immersing yourself in nature is a wonderful way to start your day with a sense of connection and gratitude.

Calm Preparation: Avoid rushing into the day. Allow yourself plenty of time to prepare in peace, whether it's selecting your attire or organizing your workspace.

Set an Intention: Before you launch into your activities, set an intention for the day. It could be a word, phrase, or sentiment that you want to nurture throughout the day.

Morning Appreciation: Upon waking up, take a moment to express gratitude for another day. Appreciating the start of a new day can boost your sense of personal value.

Significant Ritual: Create a morning ritual that has personal significance for you. It could involve lighting a candle, dancing briefly, or any activity that centers and connects you.

The key to intentional mornings is to choose practices that align with your needs and values. There is no one-size-fits-all formula, so it's important to experiment with different practices to find what resonates best with you. Starting your day with self-compassion and intention lays a strong foundation for facing the day's challenges with self-love and confidence.

Nourishing Sustenance

The way you eat plays a pivotal role in your overall well-being. Taking care of your nourishment is an act of self-love that not only sustains your physical health, but also has a profound impact on your mental and emotional health. Nutritious nourishment is a tangible way to show yourself respect and cultivate self-love. Here are some ways to seamlessly weave wholesome nourishment into the tapestry of your daily existence:

Conscious Gastronomy: Engage in mindful eating by paying attention to the hunger and fullness cues your body sends you. Savor each bite, eating slowly and deliberately, while embracing the flavors, textures, and aromas of the food.

Nutritional Equilibrium: Aim for a well-rounded dietary pattern that includes a variety of foods from different food groups: vegetables, fruits, lean protein, whole grains, and healthy fats. This ensures that you're getting the nutrients your body needs.

Adequate Hydration: Drink water throughout the day to stay hydrated. Proper hydration is essential for the body's optimal functioning and can also impact energy levels and cognitive clarity.

Intuitive Nourishment: Listen to your body and its preferences. Practice intuitive eating, a way of eating where you honor your body's signals and make food choices based on your individual needs.

Avoid Draconian Constraints: Avoid overly restrictive diets, as they can lead to feelings of deprivation. Instead, focus on adding nutritious and varied foods to your diet.

Revel in Diversity: Experiment with different foods and recipes to ensure variety in your diet. This not only ensures that you're getting a balanced intake of nutrients, but it can also make your meals more enjoyable.

Portion Control: Pay attention to the portion sizes you're eating. Eating reasonable portions will help you avoid overeating and can help you develop a healthy relationship with food.

Mindful Consumption: Avoid eating while you're doing other activities, such as working or watching TV. Focus on your meal and savor each bite.

Sidestep Appraisals: Don't judge yourself while you're eating. Avoid labeling foods as "good" or "bad." Instead, focus on making choices that are in line with your health and wellness goals.

Culinary Ventures at Home: Cooking at home gives you control over the ingredients and preparation of your food. It can also be a relaxing and creative outlet.

Integration of Nutrient-Rich Foods: Incorporate nutrient-dense foods, such as leafy green vegetables, fresh fruits, nuts, and seeds, into your meals. These foods are packed with vitamins, minerals, and antioxidants.

Grant Yourself Indulgences: Enjoy foods that bring you pleasure on occasion. Allowing for moderate indulgences is a part of the balance that is essential to self-love.

Shun Comparisons: Don't compare your eating habits to others. Everyone has different needs and preferences.

Nutrition and Emotion: Be aware of how specific foods affect your emotional state. Some foods can have a positive impact on your mood and energy levels, while others may cause fluctuations.

Healthy eating is a lifelong journey. The goal is to find a dietary pattern that works for you and promotes physical and emotional well-being. Taking care of your diet is a powerful way to nurture self-love and foster a healthy relationship with your body and mind.

Engaging in a Regimen of Movement

Regular physical activity is one of the most effective ways to take care of yourself. In addition to strengthening your physical body, it can also have a cascade of cognitive and emotional benefits. Finding a form of movement that you enjoy and that aligns with your personal preferences is essential for boosting self-esteem and creating a healthy lifestyle. Here are some things to consider as you approach regular exercise:

Choose Activities that Bring You Joy: The key to sustaining an exercise regimen is to choose activities that you truly enjoy. This will make exercise more pleasurable and will help you stick with it over the long term. Whether you prefer a leisurely walk outdoors, the gracefulness of yoga, the rhythm of running, the aquatic embrace of swimming, the expressiveness of dance, or the challenge of strength training, finding something that makes you feel good is essential.

Physical Benefits: Regular exercise can improve cardiovascular health, strengthen muscles, increase flexibility, and help you maintain a healthy weight. It can also improve blood circulation, which is essential for the smooth functioning of your body's systems.

Endorphins and Mental Well-Being: Exercise releases endorphins, which are biochemical substances that act as natural painkillers and can improve mood. This can help to reduce stress, anxiety, and depression, and can promote a more positive mental state.

Stress Reduction: Exercise is an effective way to relieve stress. When you exercise, your body releases endorphins, which have mood-boosting effects. Exercise can also help you to clear your mind and to focus on the present moment.

Energy and Vitality: Contrary to popular belief, exercise can actually increase energy levels. Over time, regular exercise can help you to feel more energized and to have more stamina.

Cultivating Consistency: The key to establishing an exercise routine is to be consistent. Start with small steps and gradually increase the intensity and duration of your workouts. Consistency is essential for reaping the benefits of exercise over time.

Variety is Key: To avoid boredom and to challenge your body in different ways, try to incorporate a variety of exercises into your routine. This could include anything from walking and running to yoga and weightlifting.

Listen to Your Body: While the benefits of exercise are undeniable, it's important to listen to your body and to respect your limits. Don't push yourself too hard or to the point of pain. If you have any pre-existing medical conditions, it's always a good idea to talk to your doctor before starting a new exercise program.

Infuse Movement into Your Daily Life: You don't have to go to the gym to get exercise. There are many ways to incorporate movement into your daily routine, such as taking the stairs instead of the elevator, walking or biking to work, or getting up and moving around every 20-30 minutes.

Celebrate Your Achievements: Just like any other accomplishment, it's important to celebrate your exercise achievements. Whether you've reached a running goal, mastered a new yoga pose, or simply stuck with your exercise routine for a month, give yourself a pat on the back.

Exercise should not be a source of stress, but rather a way to take care of yourself. Finding joy in the activities you choose and acknowledging the physical and cognitive benefits of movement are essential for nurturing self-esteem.

Interludes of Repose

Rest is an essential part of self-care and holistic well-being. Getting enough sleep and taking breaks throughout the day can help to replenish your physical and mental energy reserves. Here are some tips for incorporating interludes of repose into your daily life:

Get Enough Sleep: Sleep is essential for physical and mental health. During sleep, your body repairs itself, your brain consolidates memories, and your immune system gets a boost. Most adults need around 7-8 hours of sleep per night.

Establish a Regular Sleep Schedule: Go to bed and wake up at the same time each day, even on weekends. This will help to regulate your body's natural sleep-wake cycle.

Create a Relaxing Bedtime Routine: This could include taking a warm bath, reading a book, or listening to calming music. Avoid watching TV or using electronic devices in the hour before bed, as the blue light emitted from these devices can interfere with sleep.

Take Breaks Throughout the Day: Get up and move around every 20-30 minutes to avoid sitting for long periods of time. Take a few minutes to stretch, walk around, or do some light exercises.

Avoid Digital Distractions: When you're taking a break, try to disconnect from electronic devices and focus on the present moment. This could mean reading a book, taking a walk in nature, or spending time with your loved ones.

Engage in Soothing Activities: Find activities that help you to relax and de-stress. This could include listening to music, practicing yoga or meditation, or taking a bath.

Learn to Say No: It's important to set boundaries and protect your time for rest. If you're feeling overwhelmed, don't be afraid to say no to new commitments.

Value Your Downtime: Remember that rest is not a luxury, but a necessity. Make time for yourself each day to relax and recharge.

By prioritizing interludes of repose, you can show yourself some self-love and improve your overall well-being.

Leisure Pursuits

Life is a journey to be savored and treasured, and one of the best ways to do this is by devoting time to leisure pursuits that bring joy, contentment, and creativity into your daily routine. Immersing yourself in cherished hobbies and interests is an essential way to cultivate self-love and attend to the intricacies of your mental and emotional well-being. Here are some of the benefits of leisure pursuits:

Discovering Your Passions: Set aside some time to explore different activities and find out what truly lights your fire. Reflect on those activities that you once held dear, and consider new interests that you've been wanting to try. Embarking on this journey of discovery is a great way to reconnect with your authentic self.

Disentangling from Duties: Engaging in leisure pursuits gives you the opportunity to detach from the rigors and responsibilities of everyday life. It creates a sanctuary in your mind, a mental space where you can relax, have fun, and rejuvenate your energy.

Cultivating Creativity: Many leisure pursuits involve an element of creativity. Whether you enjoy painting, writing, cooking, or any other form of artistic expression, these activities can help you tap into your creative side and connect with your inner essence.

Mitigating Stress and Anxiety: Engaging in activities that are meaningful to you can be an effective way to reduce stress and anxiety. They offer a healthy escape from the stresses of everyday life, allowing you to focus on the present moment and temporarily let go of your worries.

Elevating Mental Well-Being: Leisure is not just about having fun; it's also a way to improve your mental health. When you pursue activities that you love, your brain releases dopamine, a neurotransmitter that is associated with feelings of pleasure and satisfaction.

Alignment with Your Authentic Self: Engaging in pursuits that you hold dear can help you to feel more authentic and purposeful. It's a way to reconnect with the essence of who you are, beyond the roles and responsibilities that you play in society.

Quality Time for Yourself: Making time for leisure is a reminder that you deserve to take care of yourself. When you make these moments special, you are strengthening your connection to your own being and expressing self-love.

Learning and Growing: Hobbies can also be a great way to learn new things and grow as a person. Mastering a new skill or developing your existing talents can boost your self-esteem and give you a sense of accomplishment.

Forging Bonds with Kindred Spirits: Participating in groups or clubs that align with your interests can help you to connect with kindred spirits who share your passions. These social interactions can enrich your life and help you to create meaningful connections.

Don't Forget to Have Fun!: Sometimes, leisure pursuits are simply about enjoying yourself and letting loose. Give yourself permission to revel in the mirth and buoyancy that these moments can bring.

Leisure pursuits are not a luxury; they are a necessity for nurturing your soul and fostering a healthy sense of self-love. Make time for these pursuits regularly, regardless of how busy you are. Your emotional and mental well-being deserve the joy and satisfaction that come from the activities that you love.

Mindfulness Practice

Modern life often pulls us in many different directions at once, leading to scattered thoughts, anxiety, and a sense of detachment. The practice of mindfulness offers a powerful way to cultivate unwavering attention to the present moment, fostering a profound sense of tranquility and self-connection. Let's take a closer look at how the art of mindfulness can be a valuable tool for nurturing self-love and well-being:

Profound Present Moment Awareness: Mindfulness is the practice of paying attention to what is happening in the present moment, without judgment. By attending to every sensation, thought, and emotion as they arise, we become attuned to our internal and external experience.

Mitigation of Stress and Anxiety: Regular mindfulness practice has been linked to the reduction of stress and anxiety. By anchoring ourselves in the present moment, we can step out of the cycle of ruminative thoughts about the past or future, and welcome in a sense of calm.

Savoring the Sublime in the Subtle: Through mindfulness, we learn to find joy and contentment in life's simplest moments. This might include appreciating the beauty of nature, savoring a quiet moment of contemplation, or immersing ourselves fully in the experience of a meal.

Self-Awareness and Self-Connection: Consistent mindfulness practice cultivates a heightened awareness of our thoughts, feelings, and physical sensations. This fosters a deeper connection with ourselves, allowing us to better understand our needs and desires.

Acceptance and Compassion: The fundamental attitude of mindfulness is acceptance. By allowing thoughts and feelings to arise without judgment, we can cultivate a more compassionate relationship with ourselves. This can reduce self-criticism and foster a more loving attitude towards ourselves.

Diminishing the Churn of Rumination: Rumination, the compulsive repetition of negative thoughts, can undermine self-love. Mindfulness practice can help to disrupt this pattern by allowing us to observe our thoughts without getting entangled in them.

Enhancing Concentration: Mindfulness requires focus and concentration. As we refine these skills through practice, we may notice an improvement in our ability to concentrate in other areas of our lives as well.

Response Over Reaction: Mindfulness practice empowers us to become more aware of our automatic reactions to challenging situations. This creates space for us to choose a more deliberate and balanced response, rather than being swept away by impulsivity.

Embracing Change and Impermanence: Mindfulness teaches us that all things are transient and in constant flux. This can help us to confront life's changes with greater resilience and acceptance.

Integration into Daily Life: The practice of mindfulness can be seamlessly integrated into our daily activities, such as walking, eating, showering, or simply breathing.

This makes mindfulness a natural and accessible part of our routine.

Mindfulness practice does not require a special environment or a lot of time. You can start with just a few minutes a day, gradually increasing your practice as you become more comfortable. By cultivating the art of being fully present in the moment, you can nourish self-love, foster emotional well-being, and discover an oasis of tranquility amid life's chaos.

Moments of Self-Care

In the midst of the ceaseless demands and distractions of modern life, carving out time for oneself is an act of essential self-care. Allocating a daily space for solitude is not merely a luxury but a fundamental necessity to nurture your inner self and cultivate self-love. Here are some ways in which "moments for oneself" can be a transformative practice:

Profound Self-Discovery: When you withdraw from the external clamor and create a haven for inner silence, you allow yourself to delve into your own mind and heart at a deeper level. This time provides an invitation to get to know yourself better, to understand your motivations, desires, and fears.

Rejuvenation of Vitality: Setting aside a moment for oneself is like recharging one's emotional batteries. It helps to alleviate accumulated stress, revitalizing the mind and spirit to face the demands of the day ahead.

Self-Connection and Intuition: By giving yourself a tranquil and introspective interval, you strengthen your connection with your intuition and inner wisdom. Oftentimes, the answers you seek are already within you, and this time allows you to heed them.

Augmentation of Creativity: Time dedicated to yourself can also serve as fertile soil for creativity to flourish. When you allow yourself a space free from distractions, inspiration and new ideas can emerge.

Stress Alleviation: In a busy world, a "moment for oneself" serves as a balm for accumulated stress. Silence and serenity provide a counterpoint to the hustle and bustle of life.

Spiritual Enrichment: For those interested in spiritual growth, moments of solitude can be an opportunity to explore practices such as prayer, contemplation, or connection with the higher self.

Self-Love and Self-Valuation: The act of reserving exclusive time for oneself tangibly demonstrates self-love. It is a declaration that you deserve this time of attention and care.

Avoidance of Burnout: Being overwhelmed by obligations and responsibilities can lead to burnout. Time for oneself acts as an antidote to such exhaustion, enabling you to recuperate and strengthen.

Cultivation of Self-Love: Self-love is an ongoing relationship with oneself. Regularly setting aside time to be with yourself is a powerful way to nurture this relationship and remind yourself of your intrinsic worth.

To create moments for oneself, it is essential to establish healthy boundaries and communicate your needs to others. Clearly define this time as non-negotiable and protect it as you would any important commitment. Whether it be a brief morning meditation, a serene sunset stroll, or a few minutes before bed to reflect on the day, this daily practice nurtures your connection with yourself and fosters authenticity, self-connection, and self-love.

Embark on the Path of Learning

The journey of learning is an endless and rewarding one that fosters personal growth and expands the boundaries of the mind. When you dedicate time to consistently acquire new knowledge, you invest in yourself in a profoundly meaningful way. Here are some ways in which the never-ending pursuit of learning contributes to your journey of self-love and personal development:

Self-Expansion: The pursuit of acquiring new knowledge or skills challenges the mind and broadens its horizons. You put yourself in situations where the acquisition of new insights or competencies is essential, a crucial part of personal evolution.

Self-Assurance: Attaining newfound skills or knowledge heightens your self-assurance. With each accomplishment, you acknowledge your ability to face challenges and overcome them victoriously.

Sense of Fulfillment: Every instance of acquiring new knowledge engenders a sense of fulfillment and contentment. These small triumphs fortify a positive self-perception.

Mental Stimulation: Learning keeps your mind alert and agile, a prerequisite for mental well-being and a deterrent against cognitive decline as you age.

Present-Moment Focus: Learning something new necessitates your undivided attention and a focus on the present. This mirrors mindfulness practice as you immerse yourself fully in the activity.

Connection with Passions: In exploring subjects that intrigue you, you forge connections with your personal passions and interests. This is a direct expression of self-love, as you allocate time to things that bring you joy.

Creative Impetus: Exposure to new ideas and knowledge can kindle your creativity. Continuous learning may lead to new avenues of creative expression in your life.

Practical Proficiency: By acquiring new knowledge, you can gain practical skills applicable across various domains of your life. This might range from mastering new culinary recipes to acquiring fluency in a new language.

Adaptation to Change: Life is an ever-evolving tapestry, and the acquisition of new insights aids in adapting to diverse scenarios and situations. This contributes to your resilience and your ability to face challenges.

Broadening of Horizons: The constant pursuit of learning exposes you to distinct viewpoints, cultures, and ideas. This broadens your perspectives and fosters empathy for diverse experiences.

Learning need not be overly complicated. It can be as simple as immersing oneself in an intriguing article, watching a documentary, attempting a new culinary recipe, or acquiring mastery over a musical instrument. The key is to keep the mind receptive and curious, seizing opportunities to learn and grow. Each incremental step you take towards perpetual learning is an investment in yourself, an embodiment of self-love, and a testament to personal appreciation.

Boundaries and the Art of Asserting No

The art of setting healthy boundaries and gracefully declining is an exercise in self-discipline and self-respect. While it may pose challenges, it stands as a crucial cornerstone for nurturing emotional well-being and overall harmony. By delineating clear boundaries in your interactions with others, you armor yourself against circumstances that might otherwise encroach upon your vitality and joy. Here are some ways in which the practice of establishing boundaries and saying no contributes to self-love:

Autonomy and Empowerment: The act of defining healthy boundaries is an assertion of empowerment. It places you at the helm of your choices and decisions, allowing you to prioritize your needs without being beholden to the desires of others.

Preservation of Energy: Setting boundaries safeguards your emotional energy. It ensures that you're not depleting yourself by constantly catering to the desires of others or engaging in activities that don't serve your well-being.

Self-valuation: The practice of boundaries is a testament to your acknowledgment of your intrinsic value. It's a proclamation that you deserve respect and that your needs and boundaries hold equal significance.

Prevention of Resentment: By setting limits, you avoid commitments and circumstances that could lead to feelings of resentment. Saying no when necessary prevents the accumulation of negative emotions.

Self and Mutual Respect: Setting healthy boundaries is an act of self-respect and respect for others. It establishes a foundation for more balanced and harmonious relationships, where the needs of all parties are taken into account.

Enhancement of Relationships: While it might seem that setting boundaries could instigate conflicts, it often actually improves relationships. When you communicate your boundaries clearly and respectfully, others learn to honor your needs and limitations.

Open Communication: Establishing healthy boundaries necessitates open communication. This fosters a more transparent and candid relationship with others, wherein you feel at ease expressing your needs and expectations.

Self-Knowledge Development: The practice of setting boundaries requires self-awareness. It helps you understand your own needs and identify situations that could be detrimental to you.

Authentic Connection: Relationships based on healthy boundaries are more authentic and genuine. You're not pretending to be someone you're not to appease others, but rather relating in a truthful and genuine manner.

Wellness Advocacy: Saying no when appropriate is a means of safeguarding yourself against circumstances that might compromise your emotional well-being. You're prioritizing your mental and emotional health.

Setting healthy boundaries is not self-centered; on the contrary, it is an essential self-care practice. It is a direct demonstration of self-love, where you put yourself first to ensure a life lived in balance and authenticity. By cultivating the art of setting boundaries and asserting yourself when necessary, you strengthen your relationship with yourself and lay a solid foundation for healthier, more fulfilling relationships.

Creative Expression

Creative expression is a powerful way to nurture your relationship with yourself. Through various avenues, such as writing, music, art, or dance, you can commune with your deepest emotions, delve into your thoughts, and release feelings that may have been pent up. The practice of creative expression not only provides a healthy outlet for your emotions, but it also contributes to the development of self-love in a unique way. Here are some ways in which creative expression can enrich your journey of self-discovery and growth:

Freedom of Articulation: Creative expression gives you the freedom to communicate authentically and without restraint. You can express your thoughts, emotions, and perspectives in your own unique way, free from external judgment.

Profound Self-Knowledge: When you engage in creative endeavors, you embark on a journey of self-exploration. This can help you to understand your desires, fears, aspirations, and values more deeply, fostering a heightened sense of self-awareness.

Release of Suppressed Emotions: Oftentimes, difficult or complex emotions are suppressed. Creative expression offers a safe and healthy way to release these emotions, allowing you to address them in a productive way.

Fostering Self-Reflection: Through creative expression, you can reflect on your experiences, beliefs, and thought patterns. This can promote ongoing self-reflection, which is essential for personal growth.

Promoting Emotional Well-Being: Engaging in creative activities can effectively enhance your emotional well-being. Activities such as painting, writing, or playing an instrument can release endorphins and boost feelings of accomplishment.

Escape from Stress: Creative expression can provide a healthy escape from the stresses and pressures of everyday life. When you immerse yourself in a creative activity, you can temporarily disconnect from your worries and focus on the present moment.

Boosting Self-Esteem: Seeing your creations come to life can boost your self-esteem. The recognition of your creative abilities and the sense of accomplishment can contribute to a positive self-image.

Cultivating Resilience: Creative experimentation often involves trial and error. By facing challenges during the creative process, you can foster resilience and the ability to navigate uncertainty.

Expressing Complex Emotions: Sometimes, words cannot adequately convey complex emotions. Creative expression offers an alternative way to articulate feelings that may be difficult to explain otherwise.

Exploring Fresh Perspectives: Through artistic creation, you can explore diverse viewpoints. This can lead to profound insights about both yourself and the world around you.

Creative expression does not require special skills or artistic talent. The goal is not to create something flawless, but rather to authentically explore your emotions and thoughts. Whether through painting, writing, music, or any other creative form that resonates with you, this practice is a valuable way to cultivate self-love, release emotions, and foster self-reflection on your path of personal growth.

Positive Social Bonds

The relationships we nurture weave an intricate tapestry, profoundly shaping how we perceive ourselves and experience selfhood. Cultivating positive social connections is a cornerstone of nurturing and fortifying self-love. These relationships do not merely contribute to our emotional well-being, but they also significantly influence our self-esteem, confidence, and sense of belonging. Here are some ways in which relationships can be harnessed to enhance our relationship with ourselves:

Discerning Selection: Choose relationships with people who value and respect you. Relationships built on mutual respect, empathy, and support are most conducive to self-esteem.

Positive Atmosphere: Healthy relationships foster an emotionally uplifting atmosphere. Surrounding yourself with people who encourage, celebrate your achievements, and bolster your aspirations contributes to a positive mindset.

Unconditional Acceptance: Authentic relationships are built on a foundation of mutual acceptance. Feeling embraced and loved by your authentic self strengthens self-acceptance and self-love.

Mutual Growth: Positive relationships encourage personal growth. Friends who share similar interests, goals, and values can propel your journey of self-development.

Shared Experiences: Spending quality time with cherished individuals facilitates shared experiences and emotions. The open expression of feelings can alleviate stress and tension, fostering self-expression.

Constructive Challenges: Healthy relationships don't shy away from challenges; they face them constructively. Conflicts resolved with respect and collaboration can fortify mutual trust and understanding.

Joint Celebrations: Genuine well-wishers genuinely rejoice in your victories, whether grand or slight. Support in accomplishments reinforces your worth and achievements.

Support in Trying Times: Authentic bonds stand firm in tough moments. Having friends or loved ones who provide a shoulder to lean on, attentive ears, and emotional support is pivotal for mental health.

Modeling Self-Care: Observing friends who practice self-care and establish healthy boundaries can inspire you to do the same. The social environment you inhabit influences your choices of self-care.

Diversity of Perspectives: Engaging with people from diverse backgrounds and perspectives can broaden your worldview. This also aids in understanding yourself better through varied interactions.

Healthy relationships require reciprocity and mutual effort. Just as you seek support and love, you must also extend the same in return. By building and nurturing positive social connections, you cultivate an environment where self-love naturally thrives. Those who surround you can serve as mirrors reflecting your positive qualities, incessantly reminding you of your intrinsic worth. Therefore, choose relationships with care and commit to their sustenance, for they play a pivotal role in your journey of growth and self-discovery.

Conscious Day Closure

The time before bed is a cherished opportunity for conscious closure, a chance to nourish your self-bond. Creating a closing ritual that encompasses reflection, gratitude, and tranquility can have a positive impact on both sleep quality and emotional well-being. Here are some eloquent ways to bid adieu to the day with purpose:

Serenity in Reflection: Find a quiet place where you can relax comfortably. Take a few moments to reflect on the ebbs and flows of the day that has passed. Revisit the moments that brought you joy, accomplishment, and self-love. Equally, pay attention to the obstacles you overcame.

Celebrate Your Triumphs: Acknowledge and celebrate your successes, no matter how small. This can help to boost your self-esteem and affirm your ability to overcome challenges.

Learn from Challenges: Consider the challenges or setbacks you encountered throughout the day. Reflect on what these situations taught you and how you can grow from these experiences.

The Grace of Gratitude: Take a moment to indulge in gratitude. Reflect on the good that came your way and express your appreciation. This can help to create a positive mental atmosphere before bed.

Liberating Worries: Before going to sleep, write down any lingering concerns or thoughts that may be weighing on your mind. This can help to release these thoughts and allow you to sleep more peacefully.

Breathing Deeply: Take several deep breaths to release tension from your body and mind. This can help to alleviate the day's accumulated stress.

Bedtime Routine: Make your bedroom a haven of rest and relaxation. This could involve adjusting the temperature, dimming the lights, and turning off electronic devices.

Nocturnal Affirmations: End your day by reciting positive affirmations. Rekindle your positive self-image before bed, recalling your intrinsic worth and power.

Affirmative Visualization: Precede sleep with a brief visualization of a peaceful and uplifting scene. This can help to calm your mind and usher in a restful sleep.

Digital Detox: Avoid using electronic devices for at least 30 minutes before going to bed. The blue light emitted by these devices can disrupt melatonin production, a hormone that regulates sleep.

The mindful practice of conscious day closure can improve the quality of your sleep and foster a more positive mindset. As the habit of reflective thought and gratitude before bed takes root, self-love will blossom, deepening your connection with yourself. Consciously closing the day not only ushers in a refreshing night's sleep, but it also primes you for a morning filled with energy and optimism.

Cultivating self-love in your everyday life is a journey of self-discovery, evolution, and transformation. It is an unwavering commitment to yourself, an investment in your mental, emotional, and spiritual well-being. As you incorporate these strategies into your daily routine and weave self-love into the fabric of your life, you will lay a foundation for positive self-esteem, healthy relationships, and a life rich with happiness and fulfillment. Remember, self-love is a daily choice, and it thrives when nourished with self-compassion, self-acceptance, and unwavering self-care.

CHAPTER 9

CONFRONTING SOLITUDE AND SELF-SUFFICIENCY

**From solitude springs dialogue
with the soul, from self-sufficiency
emerges communion with the self.**

The quest for self-love is not a linear path, and along the way, many individuals encounter intricate trials, such as solitude and self-sufficiency. These two experiences might seem paradoxical, yet both hold a profound sway over our pursuit of happiness and personal contentment. In this chapter, we shall delve into these subjects profoundly, extending insights and strategies to confront them in a wholesome and constructive manner.

NAVIGATING SOLITUDE WITH GRACE

Solitude stands as a universal human experience, and at some juncture of our lives, we each face this feeling. Solitude can materialize from various scenarios: life transitions, separations, bereavements, or simply the perception of emotional disconnection. Nonetheless, addressing solitude with grace is pivotal in safeguarding our mental and emotional well-being.

Exploring the Roots of Solitude

Solitude is an intricate and multi-faceted emotion that bears witness to the intricate labyrinth of human existence. Grasping the elusive tendrils of its underlying causes is the key to countering its effects with finesse. A mosaic of factors can contribute to the tapestry of loneliness, and dissecting these origins may offer you a compass to navigate this realm more purposefully.

Deprivation of Profound Social Bonds: Among the most prevalent roots of solitude lies the vacuum of profound, meaningful social connections. Nurturing a social sphere where understanding, value, and acceptance reverberate is the cornerstone of solitude's dismantling. Finding yourself surrounded by people yet veiled in loneliness could indicate a yearning unsated, an emotional void persisting.

Life Shifts and Transitions: Moments of seismic transformation, such as a shift in residence, the ebb of a relationship, or the bereavement of a loved one, can unfurl the carpet of solitude. Within such shifts, a sentiment of displacement and emotional unmooring may ascend. The unfamiliarity and rupture of habitual rituals can amplify the pangs of isolation.

Physical or Social Estrangement: The cloak of solitude sometimes descends through the conduits of physical or social estrangement. Instances when physical distances part you from loved ones or friends, or when social circles shut you out, a sense of exclusion envelops. The paucity of consistent social interplay over time nurtures solitude's arborescence.

Self-Altercation and Latent Self-Awareness: Solitude, it is worth noting, can equally germinate from self-disconnect. The echelons of your own emotions, yearnings, and ethos, if muffled, breed an internal solitude. The misalignment of self-awareness forges a gulf, constraining substantive connections with others.

Echoes of Trauma and Historical Vignettes: Echoes of betrayal, dismissal, or abandonment from yesteryears can cast emotional shrouds that underpin solitude's tapestry. The tempests of past scars, we find, can skew behaviors toward isolation and the bastions of self-guarding, impeding the fissures of new connections.

Professional Guidance and Insight: Should solitude endure, gnawing at your mental edifice, contemplating the embrace of professional aid, such as therapy, stands as a pivotal consideration. The hands of a skilled practitioner can guide you through the labyrinthine corridors of solitude, affording strategies to unshackle its bonds.

Confronting solitude is a journey necessitating the twin virtues of patience and self-compassion. As you untangle its origins and thread a narrative of purposeful counteraction, the tapestry of your life may flourish with meaningful bonds, nurturing a rich tapestry of emotional and social vitality.

Cultivating Genuine Connections

Embark on a quest for genuine connections to confront solitude and weave a tapestry of meaningful relationships throughout your life. These connections, like threads in a tapestry, provide a sense of belonging and mutual understanding, effectively bridging the emotional chasm often sown by solitude. Here are some artful ways to build authentic bonds:

Embrace Presence and Attentive Listening: When interacting with others, be fully present. Tune in to the symphony of their stories, genuinely show interest in their tales, and offer the balm of empathy. This art builds trust and kinship.

Unveil Your Sentiments and Chronicles: A luminous dance of reciprocity and vulnerability unfolds as you share your own thoughts and stories. The tableau you co-create encourages others to do the same, an alchemical process that can strengthen emotional bonds.

Harmonize with Group Endeavors: Participate in group activities that align with your passions. Here, you'll find a symphony of like-minded souls. This shared tapestry creates a genuine foundation for connecting with others.

Embrace Authenticity, Unveil Truth: When you reveal your authentic self, you radiate a beacon that attracts kindred spirits who value your genuine essence. Cast aside the mask of appeasement, as such guises dampen the growth of authentic relationships.

Weave Experiences into the Fabric: By weaving threads of shared moments with others, the tapestry of connection gains resonance. This can be as simple as sharing a meal, watching a movie together, or embarking on an exciting adventure.

Kindle Compassion and Mutual Support: Cultivating compassion and offering mutual support forms the bedrock of authentic connections. Be there for your loved ones when they need you, and be open to receiving support when you need it.

Forge Links Across the Digital and the Tangible: Both virtual networks and online platforms can be fertile ground for nurturing authentic connections. However, remember that the physical world, where souls can commune in person, is equally valuable. Strike a harmonious balance between these realms.

Sculpt Relationships Deliberately: Profound and meaningful relationships are sculpted over time's patient anvil. Trust's foundation and mutual understanding require careful cultivation. Be patient with your efforts, and invest your energy thoughtfully in nurturing these authentic connections.

Celebrate the Diversity in Bonds: As you master the art of fostering authentic connections, it is important to honor the diversity within relationships. Each person contributes a unique hue to the mosaic, enriching your own understanding of life. Embracing diversity invites all to a sanctuary where their worth is acknowledged and their essence is celebrated.

The Acolyte of Self-Knowledge: While traversing the terrain of authentic connections, it is essential to embark on a parallel journey of self-knowledge. Self-awareness helps you form healthy boundaries, identify relationships that align with your values, and avoid toxic entanglements. This alchemical embrace of self-infused wisdom yields authentic connections that resonate with your true essence.

Fortifying Existing Relationships

In addition to seeking new connections, it is also important to invest in strengthening the relationships that are already in your life. Strong friendships and close family ties can provide a buffer against solitude. Here are some ways to nurture and strengthen these bonds:

Encourage Open Communication: Communication is the foundation of any healthy relationship. Make sure that you keep the lines of communication open with your friends and family, sharing your thoughts, feelings, and concerns.

Spend Quality Time Together: Quality time is more important than quantity time. Make time for meaningful activities with your loved ones, such as deep conversations, shared experiences, or simply being together.

Practice Empathy: Put yourself in another person's shoes and try to understand their perspective. Empathy builds bridges of understanding and strengthens connections.

Express Gratitude and Appreciation: Let your loved ones know how much you appreciate them. Express your thanks for their presence and contributions to your life.

Be there for Each Other in Times of Need: Be a source of support for your loved ones when they need you. Be a listening ear and offer practical help when possible.

Celebrate Each Other's Successes: Share in each other's joy when they achieve their goals. Celebrate their accomplishments and help them to feel proud of their successes.

Resolve Conflict Constructively: Conflict is a natural part of any relationship. When conflict arises, it is important to handle it in a respectful and constructive way. Learn to listen to each other without judgment and to communicate your needs clearly.

Perform Acts of Kindness: Small acts of kindness can have a big impact. Send a thoughtful message, plan a surprise, or offer help when needed.

Adapt to Change: People and relationships change over time. Be open to change and be willing to grow and evolve together.

Respect Individuality: Honor each person's unique perspective and experiences. Mutual respect is essential for maintaining healthy relationships.

Identify Toxic Relationships: As you strengthen your existing relationships, it is important to be aware of toxic relational patterns. Relationships that are characterized by emotional abuse, manipulation, or disrespect are unhealthy and can contribute to feelings of isolation. If you identify any patterns of harmful behavior, it is important to set boundaries or even end the relationship.

Balance Self-Sufficiency with Relationships: While it is important to invest in your relationships, it is also important to maintain a healthy degree of self-sufficiency. Don't rely on others to meet all of your emotional needs.

Remember to take care of yourself and pursue activities that bring you joy and fulfillment. This balance will help you to build strong relationships and to cope with solitude in a healthy way.

Embark on the Practice of Vulnerability

Oftentimes, the tendrils of solitude can prompt us to emotionally withdraw, driven by the fear of potential rejection or judgment. However, engaging in the art of vulnerability is a key step towards overcoming this sense of isolation. Vulnerability is the sharing of our authentic thoughts and feelings with others, even if it can be scary. Here are some reasons why the practice of vulnerability is an essential ally in grappling with loneliness:

Forging Authentic Bonds: When we allow ourselves to be vulnerable, we invite others to do the same. This creates the foundation for relationships that are deep and meaningful, where we can truly connect with each other on an emotional level.

Diminishing the Veil of Isolation: Loneliness often arises when we feel like our emotions are solitary, or when we believe that no one truly understands our inner world. When we share our emotions with others, we realize that we are not alone in our experiences.

Incubating Empathy: When we reveal our vulnerabilities, we create a fertile ground for others to understand the intricacies of their own emotions. This nurtures empathy and mutual understanding.

Challenging Confining Beliefs: Engaging in vulnerability challenges the limiting belief that vulnerability is a sign of weakness. In fact, it takes courage and authenticity to be vulnerable.

Nurturing Self-Acceptance: Sharing our experiences and emotions helps us to validate ourselves. This, in turn, contributes to self-acceptance and a more positive self-image.

Paving the Path for Support: When we embrace vulnerability, we open the door to support and encouragement from others. Those in our circle can offer solace, guidance, and invaluable perspectives.

Nurturing Vulnerability Gradually: The cultivation of vulnerability is not always an easy feat, especially if we are not accustomed to sharing our emotions openly. It is important to start slowly and comfortably, choosing trusted individuals with whom we feel comfortable being vulnerable. Here are a few tips for practicing vulnerability in a healthy way:

Choose the Right Moment: Choose a time when you are feeling calm and relaxed, and when you have plenty of time to talk.

Be Authentic: Share your true thoughts and feelings, without hiding or downplaying anything.

Start Small: Start by sharing fewer personal thoughts and feelings, and gradually work your way up to more intimate topics.

Be a Good Listener: When someone shares their vulnerabilities with you, be sure to listen actively and with empathy.

Accept Different Reactions: Not everyone will react to your vulnerability in the same way. Some people may be supportive, while others may be uncomfortable. It is important to accept different reactions without taking them personally.

Remember That You Are Not Alone: Everyone experiences challenges and difficult emotions at different points in their lives. Sharing your vulnerabilities can help to create a community of support.

The practice of vulnerability takes time and effort, but it is a powerful tool for overcoming loneliness and building meaningful relationships.

Discovering Solace Amid Solitude

While seeking connections is essential for addressing loneliness, it is also important to learn how to find solace in solitude itself. Nurturing self-compassion and engaging in pursuits that bring you joy when you are alone can be effective ways to alleviate the pain of loneliness. Finding delight and meaning in your own company can be transformative. Here are some ways to find solace in solitude:

Cultivate Self-Compassion: Self-compassion is about treating yourself with the same kindness and understanding that you would extend to a close friend. When you feel lonely, practice self-compassion by reminding yourself that everyone experiences solitude at times.

Engage in Self-Exploration: Use solitary moments to delve deeper into your own inner world. Self-exploration is a journey of uncovering your desires, values, and passions. The more you get to know yourself, the more connected you will become to your own essence.

Foster Personal Hobbies and Passions: Take up pursuits that genuinely captivate you and can be enjoyed alone. This could include reading, writing, cooking, painting, playing a musical instrument, or practicing yoga. Taking pleasure in these endeavors will strengthen your relationship with yourself.

Create Moments of Self-Care: Turn solitude into opportunities for self-care. Indulge in a relaxing bath, take a walk in nature, meditate, or simply unwind with a cup of tea. These pockets of self-care will nourish both your mind and body.

Practice Mindfulness Amid Solitude: When you are ensconced in solitude, practice mindfulness. Immerse yourself in the sensations, thoughts, and emotions of the present moment, letting go of attachment to past or future concerns. This will cultivate a love for the present moment.

Cultivate Imagination and Creativity: Use solitary hours to explore the realms of your imagination and creativity. Write, sketch, create stories, or simply allow yourself to daydream. These endeavors will stimulate your intellect and bring a sense of accomplishment.

Seek Intentional Solitude: Instead of avoiding solitude, actively seek it out from time to time. Solitude can provide a canvas for profound reflection and tranquility, allowing you to reconnect with yourself.

Harbor Gratitude for Your Own Company: Just as you express gratitude for external things, extend gratitude for your own company. Acknowledge the qualities and attributes that make you unique and valuable.

Moderate Technology Overindulgence: While technology can serve as a virtual bridge, excessive reliance on it can paradoxically amplify the feeling of loneliness. Set aside time each day to be free of electronic devices so that you can truly bask in your own presence.

Finding solace in solitude does not mean isolating yourself from the world. Instead, it is about embracing the opportunity to forge a meaningful connection with your inner being. By fostering a healthy relationship with your own company, you will not only navigate loneliness in a more wholesome way, but you will also enrich your inner life and build a strong foundation of self-love.

Embracing Social Engagements

Engaging in social activities and groups that resonate with your interests and values is an effective way to combat loneliness and build meaningful relationships. In doing so, you not only have the chance to meet new people, but you also feel connected to a community that shares your passions. Here are some strategies for engaging in social activities in a healthy way:

Identify Your Passions: Reflect on activities or hobbies that genuinely spark your excitement. This could include sports, artistic pursuits, reading clubs, cooking classes, volunteer groups, and more. Choose activities that bring you joy.

Research Local Groups and Events: Explore the available options in your community. Use social media, local websites, and bulletin boards to find groups and events that align with your interests. There are often groups dedicated to specific hobbies, social causes, and cultural endeavors.

Participate in Classes or Workshops: Enrolling in classes or workshops is a great way to connect with people while also learning new skills. In addition to acquiring new skills, you'll have the opportunity to interact with peers who share your interest in the subject matter.

Frequent Public Spaces: Cafes, libraries, parks, and cultural centers are all places where you might cross paths with people who are also looking for social interaction. Be open to starting conversations with people who seem receptive.

Engage in Support Groups: If you are facing specific challenges in your life, such as recent changes, mental health issues, or health problems, consider joining a support group. These groups offer a safe space to share experiences and build meaningful connections.

Volunteer: Volunteering is a rewarding way to connect with your community while also making a positive impact. Choose an organization or cause that resonates with you and devote your time to helping others. This is also a great way to meet people who share your values.

Participate in Online Social Events: In addition to in-person activities, there are many social groups and events happening online. Engage in webinars, discussion forums, or social media groups that focus on your areas of interest.

Initiate Open Conversations: When participating in these activities, be open to starting conversations with new acquaintances. Ask about their interests, share your own experiences, and show genuine curiosity in getting to know the people around you.

Maintain Consistency: To build meaningful relationships, it's important to maintain a consistent involvement in the activities. Attend meetings or events regularly so that people can start to recognize you and build stronger bonds.

Engaging in social activities can help to dispel loneliness and enrich your life by providing an opportunity to exchange experiences, learn from others, and build genuine connections. It's normal to take some time to feel fully comfortable and connected in new groups, but the effort is worthwhile as you begin to reap the emotional and social rewards.

The Significance of Authenticity

When it comes to addressing solitude in a healthy way, authenticity is a key trait that can have a profound impact on your relationships and emotional well-being. To be authentic is to be true to yourself and to others, giving yourself permission to express your feelings, thoughts, and needs in a genuine manner. Here are some of the benefits of authenticity:

Cultivating Meaningful Connections: Authenticity is a magnet for genuine relationships. When you are authentic, you attract people who value you for who you are, not for who you try to be to please others. This paves the way for deeper, more meaningful connections, where you can share real experiences and feel truly understood.

Self-Acceptance and Self-Esteem: Through authenticity, you embrace yourself with all your imperfections and qualities. This lays the foundation for strong self-acceptance and boosts your self-esteem. You acknowledge that you are worthy of love and belonging, regardless of external expectations.

Resilience Against Solitude: Authenticity can also help you combat loneliness. When you are willing to share your vulnerabilities and needs with others, you create space for them to reciprocate. This nurtures an environment of mutual trust, where loneliness can dissipate through understanding and support.

Reduction of Stress and Anxiety: Striving to maintain a facade or conceal your true self can be stressful and draining. Authenticity allows you to liberate yourself from masks and the pressures of pretending to be someone you're not. This leads to a reduction in stress and anxiety, as you no longer need to constantly worry about upholding a false appearance.

Personal Growth and Self-Knowledge: Authenticity requires self-awareness and self-reflection. By exploring and sharing your own feelings and experiences, you become more attuned to yourself and your values. This fosters ongoing personal growth as you learn more about who you are and what you aspire to in life.

Inspiration for Others: Your authenticity can inspire those around you. When you have the courage to be true to yourself, you show others that it is possible to live an authentic and fulfilling life, even if it means challenging societal norms or expectations.

Support in Challenges: During difficult times, authenticity empowers you to seek support and understanding. By authentically sharing your struggles and difficulties, you create a space for others to offer assistance, advice, or simply a listening ear.

Authenticity is not an instantaneous process; it is an ongoing journey of self-exploration and genuine expression. There may be moments when you feel apprehensive about being authentic, especially if it involves vulnerability. However, the emotional benefits and the establishment of meaningful relationships make the effort worthwhile. By choosing authenticity, you are opting for a life enriched with genuine connections and self-acceptance.

AVOIDING THE SNARE OF EXCESSIVE SELF-SUFFICIENCY

While self-sufficiency is a valuable quality, excessive self-sufficiency can become an emotional snare. When we become overly self-sufficient, we resist seeking help or emotionally connecting with others. This can lead to emotional solitude and a lack of support during challenging times.

The Roots of Excessive Self-Sufficiency

Excessive Self-Sufficiency is a behavioral pattern that can have profound emotional and psychological roots. Often, these roots develop from past experiences, limiting beliefs, and coping mechanisms. Possible roots of excessive self-sufficiency include:

Past Traumas: Past traumatic experiences, such as abuse, neglect, or loss, can lead to a sense of distrust in others. If you have been hurt by those close to you, you may develop a mindset that it's better to rely solely on yourself to avoid further pain.

Rejection or Abandonment: Feelings of rejection or abandonment in past relationships can foster excessive self-sufficiency. If you have been left behind or felt undervalued in the past, you might believe it's safer to rely on no one but yourself.

Beliefs of Inadequacy: Deep-seated beliefs of inadequacy can fuel self-sufficiency. If you believe you are unworthy of help or support, you might feel compelled to handle everything on your own. Such beliefs can arise from experiences of low self-esteem or constant comparisons with others.

Childhood Patterns: Childhood experiences, such as being encouraged to be independent from an early age, can contribute to excessive self-sufficiency. If you grew up in an environment where your needs weren't met or were encouraged to solve your own problems, you may internalize that message and carry it into adulthood.

Fear of Vulnerability: Excessive self-sufficiency often roots in the fear of being vulnerable. If you've learned that showing weaknesses or asking for help is a sign of weakness, you might choose to avoid vulnerability at all costs, maintaining your self-sufficiency.

Past Emotional Dependency: Some people adopt self-sufficiency as a response to previous experiences of emotional dependency. If you have previously been overly dependent on someone emotionally and suffered from it, you might opt to avoid depending on others to protect your emotional well-being.

Lack of Positive Role Models: A lack of models for healthy and balanced relationships can lead to self-sufficiency. If you didn't have examples of relationships where mutual dependency and support were valued, you might not have learned how to trust others in a healthy manner.

Recognizing the roots of excessive self-sufficiency is the first step towards addressing it in a healthy manner. As you become more aware of past experiences and beliefs that fuel this pattern, you can begin to challenge these beliefs and seek new ways to relate to yourself and others. Therapy, self-awareness, and the pursuit of healthy relationships can play a significant role in overcoming excessive self-sufficiency and building a more balanced and connected life.

The Perils of Excessive Self-Sufficiency

While self-sufficiency is a valuable skill, it is important to acknowledge that when taken to the extreme, it can entail risks and significant challenges. The risks associated with excessive self-sufficiency are as follows:

Emotional Isolation: Excessive self-sufficiency can lead to emotional isolation, where you shut yourself off from others and avoid sharing your feelings and concerns. This can result in a sense of loneliness and disconnection, as you do not allow others to get close to you emotionally.

Lack of Social Support: By avoiding reliance on others, you may deny yourself the valuable support that healthy relationships can offer. This can leave you without a social support network when facing challenges, which can amplify stress and feelings of overwhelm.

Excessive Pressure: Attempting to handle everything on your own can lead to excessive emotional and mental pressure. You may feel responsible for resolving all problems, which can lead to heightened levels of stress and burnout.

Difficulty in Seeking Help: Excessive self-sufficiency can make it challenging to ask for help when you truly need it. This can result in resistance to seeking guidance, support, or advice from others, even when it would be beneficial.

Emotional Exhaustion: The lack of emotional support and the constant pressure of being self-sufficient can lead to emotional exhaustion. Without the opportunity to share your emotions and concerns, you may feel overwhelmed and emotionally drained.

Superficial Relationships: Excessive self-sufficiency can result in superficial relationships, where you do not open up emotionally and do not allow others to glimpse the true depth of who you are. This can hinder the development of meaningful connections.

Perfectionism: The relentless pursuit of self-sufficiency can be tied to perfectionism, where you constantly strive to be independent and do everything flawlessly. This pattern can be exhausting and lead to unattainable self-demands.

Lack of Personal Growth: Excessive self-sufficiency can limit your personal growth. Healthy relationships and meaningful connections often challenge us and help us grow. By avoiding interdependence, you may miss valuable opportunities for learning and development.

Difficulty in Delegating: The need for self-sufficiency can make it hard for you to delegate tasks or trust others to assist. This can be particularly problematic in work environments or collaborations.

Barrier to Self-Love: Excessive self-sufficiency can hinder genuine self-love practice. True self-compassion involves recognizing when you need help and allowing yourself to receive support when necessary.

Recognizing these risks and challenges is crucial to finding a healthy balance between self-sufficiency and interdependence. Cultivating genuine relationships, allowing yourself to be vulnerable, and learning to trust others are important steps in avoiding the perils of excessive self-sufficiency and promoting your emotional and relational well-being.

Discovering the Balance

Navigating the equilibrium between self-sufficiency and receptivity to support is a pivotal journey of self-discovery and personal growth. Strategies and considerations that can assist you in achieving this healthy equilibrium include:

Profound Self-Awareness: Begin by cultivating profound self-awareness. Pay attention to your patterns of behavior and thought when it comes to self-reliance versus seeking assistance. Be aware of instances when you emotionally close off or resist receiving support.

Contemplate Your Needs: Dedicate time to contemplate your emotional, mental, and physical needs. Acknowledge that everyone has limitations and that it is natural to require help at certain times. Ask yourself, "What am I feeling? What do I truly need in this moment?"

Unearth Your Fears: Probe into underlying fears that might contribute to your excess of self-sufficiency. Ask yourself, "What inhibits me from asking for help?" Identifying these fears can help you to address them in a more conscious way.

Embrace Vulnerability: Vulnerability is an act of bravery. Start by practicing vulnerability in small steps. Share your thoughts or feelings with a trusted individual and observe how it affects your relationship and self-perception.

Forge Meaningful Bonds: Elevate the construction of meaningful and authentic relationships. Seek out individuals who support and value your emotional openness. These relationships provide a safe haven for you to be your authentic self.

Seek Aid When Needed: Remind yourself that seeking assistance is not a sign of weakness but rather one of courage and self-awareness. As you recognize the need for support, be open to seeking it from friends, family, therapists, or mentors.

Hone the Art of Receiving: Hone the art of receiving with gratitude. When someone extends help, embrace it wholeheartedly. Allowing others to contribute is also an act of generosity, allowing them to feel valued.

Establish Wholesome Boundaries: Striking a balance does not mean relying excessively on others. Establish healthy boundaries within your relationships so that you can receive support when necessary while also maintaining your autonomy and independence.

Celebrate Interaction: Celebrate instances when you share, connect, and allow others to enter your emotional realm. Cherish these moments as opportunities for personal growth and relationship reinforcement.

Practice Self-Kindness: Discovering balance is an ongoing journey. Do not chastise yourself for moments of excessive self-sufficiency. Practice self-kindness and acknowledge that you are in the process of growth and learning.

Achieving equilibrium between self-sufficiency and openness to receiving support is a vital step towards emotional well-being and thriving. This allows you to forge deeper connections with both yourself and others, fostering relationships that are more authentic and meaningful.

The Significance of Communication

Communication plays a pivotal role in avoiding the trap of excessive self-sufficiency. By engaging in open and honest communication, you build bridges of connection with others, strengthen your relationships, and cultivate a healthy sense of interdependence. Here are some reasons why communication is essential in this context:

Fosters Mutual Understanding: Through communication, you share your thoughts, feelings, and perspectives with others. This allows them to gain a deeper understanding of who you are and what you are experiencing, fostering greater empathy and connection.

Creates Room for Mutual Support: By revealing your needs and challenges, you create space for others to offer support and assistance. Effective communication empowers you to articulate your struggles, allowing others to stand by your side.

Strengthens Relationships: Healthy relationships are built on the foundation of communication. Through open sharing, you build trust and intimacy within your connections, nurturing an environment where everyone feels valued and understood.

Prevents Emotional Isolation: Excessive self-sufficiency can lead to emotional isolation, where you withdraw from those around you. Effective communication serves as an antidote to this isolation, allowing you to express your emotions and avoid detachment.

Cultivates the Courage of Vulnerability: Communication requires vulnerability in sharing your emotions and concerns. By practicing open communication, you foster the courage to authentically express yourself, thereby strengthening your self-esteem.

Averts Misunderstandings: Lack of communication can breed misunderstandings and resentments. By clearly and directly articulating your thoughts, you minimize the likelihood of misconceptions and unnecessary conflict.

Enhances Self-Awareness: As you share your thoughts and emotions with others, you also become more attuned to your own needs and challenges. This promotes self-authenticity.

Encourages a Cooperative Approach: Effective communication encourages a cooperative and mutually supportive approach. Rather than trying to solve everything on your own, you allow others to share their perspectives and ideas, enriching your decision-making process.

Paves the Way for Creative Solutions: In sharing challenges and issues, you may gain insights and creative solutions from others. This broadens your repertoire of resources for dealing with difficult situations.

Nurtures Meaningful Relationships: Effective communication is a cornerstone for nurturing meaningful relationships. By fostering an environment of openness and honesty, you cultivate a sense of belonging and connection.

Communication is a two-way street. In addition to expressing your own thoughts and emotions, it is also important to listen attentively to what others have to say. The ongoing practice of open and honest communication will help you avoid the pitfall of excessive self-sufficiency and promote healthy, enriching relationships.

Mastering the Art of Seeking Assistance

Embark on the journey of learning how to ask for help. It is an essential step in avoiding the trap of excessive self-reliance and navigating solitude in a healthy way. While it may be challenging, asking for help is an act of courage, humility, and self-awareness. Here are some perspectives that can help you master the art of seeking help more effectively:

Shift the Paradigm on Seeking Help: Understand that seeking help is not a sign of weakness, but rather a recognition that everyone experiences times when they need support. It takes strength and courage to ask for help when necessary.

Acknowledge Your Limitations: No one is able to do everything on their own all the time. Recognizing your own limitations shows authenticity and self-awareness. By acknowledging where you need help, you are being honest with yourself.

Identify Trusted Individuals: Find people in your life who you trust and who are willing to offer support. This could include close friends, family members, or healthcare professionals. Building a reliable support network is essential.

Be Specific About Your Needs: When asking for help, be clear about the type of support you are seeking. This will help others understand your needs and provide help more effectively.

Embrace Vulnerability: Asking for help requires vulnerability, admitting that you don't have all the answers. Embracing vulnerability is key to building authentic relationships and fostering deep connections.

Express Gratitude and Appreciation: When someone offers help, express gratitude and appreciation. This shows that you value the assistance they are providing, which will strengthen the bonds between you and them.

Foster a Culture of Mutual Support: When you ask for help when needed, you also inspire others to do the same. This creates an environment of mutual support, where everyone feels comfortable sharing their needs.

Practice Acceptance: Just as it is important to ask for help, it is also important to accept it when it is offered. Often, we resist help because of pride or the fear of burdening others. Practicing the acceptance of others' generosity is essential.

Remember Your Personal Growth: Asking for help and receiving support are avenues for your personal growth. You empower yourself to face challenges more effectively and build healthy relationships.

Celebrate Collective Triumphs: When you receive help, see it as a collective triumph, not just a temporary relief. By working together and supporting each other, we can all achieve success.

Learning how to ask for help is an ongoing process that involves practicing authenticity, humility, and openness. As you internalize the importance of seeking support when needed, you will forge deeper relationships and build emotional resilience.

Cultivating Nurturing Bonds

Nurturing supportive relationships is a key part of avoiding the pitfall of excessive self-reliance and navigating solitude in a healthy way. Authentic and meaningful connections play a vital role in our emotional well-being and vitality. Here are some strategies for cultivating nurturing bonds in your life:

Prioritize Genuine Connections: Seek out relationships with people who value you for who you are and who are willing to be there for you in times of need. Avoid superficial or toxic relationships that could undermine your self-esteem.

Share Experiences and Emotions: Foster emotional openness by sharing your experiences and emotions with trusted friends and family. This creates an environment of trust and reciprocity, where both parties can mutually support each other.

Demonstrate Empathy: Show empathy while listening to others and offering support. Show that you care about others' feelings and concerns, which will strengthen bonds and build a foundation of mutual assistance.

Be Present in Hardship: A true supportive relationship is one where individuals are there for each other in times of difficulty. Be there to lend an ear and offer support when someone is going through a tough time.

Celebrate Triumphs and Joys: Just as it is important to be there for others in difficult times, it is also important to celebrate their victories and joys. Share in the elation and accomplishments of your friends and loved ones, which shows that you care about their well-being.

Set Healthy Boundaries: Healthy relationships involve establishing boundaries that respect the needs and limitations of both parties. Communicate your own needs and be willing to honor those of others.

Communicate Openly: Open and honest communication is the foundation of any healthy relationship. Be willing to talk about your worries, feelings, and needs, and encourage others to do the same.

Offer Judgment-Free Support: When providing support, do so without judgment. Avoid criticism or unsolicited advice. Instead, listen and offer support without imposing your opinion.

Pursue Common Interests: Forge connections based on shared interests. Participating in activities or groups that align with your interests is an effective way to meet people who value what you value.

Acknowledge Individual Differences: Everyone is unique, and this includes how we give and receive support. Be open to recognizing individual differences in how people express care and support.

Be Consistent and Reliable: Reliability is a key trait in any supportive relationship. Be there when you say you will be, and follow through on your promises.

Be Willing to Forgive and Transcend Conflicts: In any relationship, disagreements may arise. Be willing to forgive, move on, and transcend conflicts, provided the relationship is healthy and worthwhile.

Cultivating nurturing relationships takes time, effort, and mutual commitment. However, the benefits are immeasurable. Authentic relationships not only help to combat loneliness, but they also contribute to your personal growth, emotional well-being, and overall happiness.

Embracing Acceptance

The practice of acceptance is an emotional journey that encompasses the recognition and embrace of one's own humanity, vulnerabilities included. Acknowledging that you need not face everything alone is a key step in avoiding the pitfalls of excessive self-reliance and fostering healthy relationships. Here are some ways to practice acceptance when it comes to your own support needs:

Emotional Self-Awareness: Start by developing emotional self-awareness. Acknowledge and identify your own feelings, without judgment. This includes emotions of loneliness, sadness, fear, or any other sentiment you may be experiencing.

Acknowledge Your Needs: It is important to accept that you have emotional needs and do not have to face challenges alone. Recognize that seeking support, comfort, and understanding is perfectly normal and human.

Cultivate Self-Compassion: Self-compassion is the art of treating oneself with the same kindness and understanding that you would extend to a dear friend. Rather than berate yourself for needing help, practice self-compassion and acknowledge that seeking support is normal.

Challenge Limiting Beliefs: Excessive self-reliance is often fueled by limiting beliefs, such as "asking for help is a sign of weakness." Challenge these beliefs by recognizing that seeking support is a sign of strength and courage.

Learn to Receive: Just as it is important to offer support, it is equally important to learn to receive it. Many self-sufficient individuals find it challenging to accept help from others. Practice graciously accepting help when it is offered.

Value Human Connections: Recognize the value of human connections. Relationships are an integral part of the human experience, offering support, solace, and a sense of belonging. Value the positive role that others can play in your life.

Cultivate Trusting Relationships: Nurturing trusting relationships is a form of practicing acceptance. When you have people you trust and can rely on, it becomes easier to accept their assistance.

Avoid Perfectionism: Perfectionism can lead to the belief that you must be capable of handling everything on your own and must not make mistakes. Remember that everyone has limitations, and making mistakes is part of growth.

Celebrate Emotional Intimacy: Practicing acceptance also means celebrating emotional intimacy. This means allowing yourself to share your deepest emotions with others and allowing them to reciprocate with you.

Foster a Supportive Environment: In your closest relationships, create an environment where expressing needs and seeking emotional support is safe. Show your availability to listen and support others.

Recall Your Humanity: You are human, and humanity is characterized by our interdependence and need for connection. Accepting help from others is an expression of our human nature.

By practicing acceptance, you recognize your own vulnerability and foster an attitude of receptivity toward receiving support. This not only strengthens your relationships, but it also bolsters your emotional health and overall well-being.

Confronting solitude in a healthy way and sidestepping the trap of excessive self-reliance are challenges that we all face at different junctures in our lives. It is important to remember that we are social and emotional beings who need connection and support. Striking a balance between independence and openness to genuine relationships is essential for preserving our mental, emotional, and overall well-being.

ATTRACTING HEALTHY RELATIONSHIPS

Like a magnet of self-love,
draw forth hearts that beat
to the same frequency.

Healthy relationships are like flowers blooming in our emotional garden, bringing beauty, joy, and growth. But attracting these meaningful connections takes more than just luck. It requires radiating positive energy, exploring self-awareness, and remaining open to love's embrace. In this chapter, we'll explore how these three facets work together to attract healthy and fulfilling relationships.

RADIATING POSITIVE ENERGIES TO DRAW KINDRED SOULS

Just as a magnet attracts objects of opposing charge, our emotional energies also play a vital role in attracting like-minded individuals. Emitting positive energy encompasses nurturing an optimistic mindset, being open to new experiences, and summoning the best within ourselves.

Cultivating a Positive Mindset

A positive mindset is like a beacon that illuminates our path, making our journey brighter and more appealing. When we make an effort to cultivate a positive mindset, we're not just improving our own quality of life, but we're also increasing our ability to attract healthy and meaningful relationships.

The Influence of Mindset on Relationship Attraction: Our mindset plays a profound role in how we connect with others. Imagine meeting someone who radiates positivity, confidence, and optimism. This person would instantly seem more attractive, because their positive energy is infectious and delightful. Healthy relationships thrive on a balanced exchange of energy, and a positive mindset can be the magnet that draws kindred spirits.

Self-Discovery and Self-Acceptance: Cultivating a positive mindset begins with self-discovery and self-acceptance. It's important to acknowledge and embrace all aspects of ourselves, imperfections included. This doesn't mean overlooking areas that need growth, but rather addressing them with self-compassion and the belief in our ability to evolve.

Focusing on Opportunities and Solutions: A positive mindset teaches us to look beyond challenges and focus on opportunities and solutions. Instead of fixating on obstacles, we channel our energy into finding ways to overcome them. This approach not only strengthens us individually, but it also creates an environment conducive to healthy relationships, where both partners are committed to facing challenges together.

Resilience and Growth: A positive mindset makes us more resilient in the face of adversity. We acknowledge that life's ebbs and flows are natural and we're willing to learn and grow from them. This adaptability not only helps us manage our own challenges, but it also allows us to be a source of support for others during their difficult times.

Attracting Compatible Individuals: When we emit positive energy, we naturally attract people who are on the same wavelength. Healthy relationships are built on mutual respect, support, and appreciation. Those who share our positive mindset are drawn to our energy, recognizing the benefits of being around someone who creates an emotionally enriching environment.

Overcoming Challenges: A positive mindset doesn't mean we're immune to challenges. Instead, it means we're prepared to face them with courage and perseverance. In relationships, this translates into a collaborative approach to problem-solving and overcoming obstacles together. A positive mindset helps us stay calm and confident even during difficult times.

Cultivating a positive mindset is an investment in our own happiness and in the quality of the relationships we attract. When we make an effort to approach life with optimism and confidence, we elevate not only our own experience, but we also create a magnet for healthy and meaningful relationships. The positive energy we emanate draws people who value our inner light and who yearn to share their own positive energy. By nurturing our positive mindset, we're paving the way for authentic and enriching connections.

Attracting Those Who Cherish Positivity

Our emotional energies are like a magnet that draws people who resonate with us. When we cultivate a state of internal well-being and radiate confidence and positivity, we create a magnetic field that draws people who share our mindset and energy. This phenomenon is an embodiment of the law of attraction, which states that like attracts like.

The Harmony of Energies: The emotions and vibrations we emit may not be visible to the eye, but they have a powerful effect on the atmosphere around us. Picture yourself entering a room full of people: you can probably sense the atmosphere, whether people are content, tense, relaxed, or animated. This ability to sense energy in our surroundings is an innate skill, often referred to as "feeling the vibe."

The Potency of Positive Vibrations: When we are in good spirits, optimistic, and self-assured, our energy exudes a positive vibration that resonates with the positivity of others. These positive energies are contagious and attractive. People who also value positivity and personal growth are naturally drawn to these vibrations. They are the ones who tend to gravitate towards us, initiating conversations, sharing interests, and fostering an atmosphere of genuine connection.

The Significance of Energetic Compatibility: Attracting people who value positivity is essential for cultivating healthy relationships. When we share a foundation of similar values and mindset with those around us, interactions become more authentic and fulfilling. This energetic compatibility allows for an authentic exchange of support, growth, and mutual learning.

Co-Creating Healthy Relationships: By drawing people who cherish positivity, we create a conducive environment for personal and relational growth. Relationships founded upon similar values, mutual respect, and emotional support are more likely to thrive. Together, we co-create a space where each individual can flourish in their unique journey, while mutually supporting each other in their aspirations and challenges.

Cultivating Positive Energies: Nurturing a positive mindset and practicing self-care are effective ways to strengthen our positive energies. When we take care of our emotional well-being, we are naturally inclined to radiate positivity. This includes practicing gratitude, maintaining optimistic thoughts, engaging in activities that bring us joy, and fostering relationships that uplift and enrich us.

The allure of people who hold positivity in high regard is an organic process that begins within ourselves. As we nurture positive energies and authenticity, we inherently establish a magnetic field that draws people who are aligned with our values and mindset. This attraction forms the foundation for building healthy relationships, where mutual support and personal growth take center stage. In our steadfast pursuit of sustaining positive energy, we are cultivating an environment conducive to authentic and meaningful connections.

Embarking on Authenticity

Being authentic is one of the most powerful cornerstones for attracting healthy and meaningful relationships. Authenticity means expressing who we are genuinely, without masks, pretense, or trying to please others. When we embody authenticity, we radiate an energy and presence that resonates with our inner truth, naturally drawing people who value this quality.

The Power of Authenticity: Authenticity is like an inner beacon that shines outward. When we present ourselves to the world as our true selves, we emit an energy that is distinctive and unmistakable. This authenticity harmonizes with other people who also value emotional honesty and genuine connection. The energy that comes from authenticity is magnetic, because it forms a strong foundation for relationships based on mutual respect and deep understanding.

Forging Profound Bonds: By expressing ourselves authentically, we open the door for others to truly know us. This vulnerability and candor creates an environment where people feel comfortable sharing their own experiences, thoughts, and emotions. Authenticity engenders genuine connection, allowing relationships to blossom on the foundation of mutual understanding and emotional support.

Attracting Like-Minded Souls: Through authenticity, we naturally attract people who are drawn to our genuine essence. This results in deeper and more meaningful relationships, where both parties can be themselves without shame. The energy of authenticity serves as a magnet for those who also seek unpretentious and genuine relationships.

The Courage of Authenticity: Being authentic takes courage. Oftentimes, we feel pressure to conform to societal norms or other people's expectations. However, when we allow ourselves to be truly authentic, we affirm our own worth and individuality. The courage to be authentic also inspires others to open up and connect on a deeper level.

Authenticity and Personal Growth: The practice of authenticity not only strengthens our external relationships, but it also fosters our own personal growth. By truly knowing ourselves and embracing our authentic selves, we cultivate self-esteem and self-confidence. This inner growth also manifests in our interactions with others, establishing a positive cycle of authentic connections and personal development.

Authenticity is a powerful tool for attracting compatible people and nurturing healthy, meaningful relationships. When we give ourselves the freedom to be authentically ourselves, we generate magnetic energy that attracts people who value sincerity, honesty, and genuine connection. The practice of authenticity not only enriches our relationships, but it also contributes to our personal growth and self-esteem. By being bold enough to be authentic, we are opening the door to authentic and meaningful relationships in our lives.

Developing an Open and Curious Approach

One of the keys to attracting healthy and enriching relationships is to cultivate an open and curious approach to others and the world around you. This mindset not only helps you connect with kindred spirits, but it also propels personal growth and the exploration of a more abundant and meaningful life.

Venturing into the Unknown: Being willing to venture into the unknown is an attitude of growth and expansion. When you open yourself up to meeting new people, cultures, ideas, and experiences, you demonstrate a desire to broaden your horizons and enrich your life. This paves the way for meaningful interactions and relationships that add value.

Stepping Beyond the Comfort Zone: The comfort zone is a place of security, but it can also be a confining space. By stepping beyond its boundaries, you allow yourself to confront challenges and embrace new endeavors. This not only strengthens your resilience, but it also puts you in situations where you can meet people who share your interests and values.

Learning from Others: An open and curious approach allows you to learn from others. Each person carries a unique perspective and a tapestry of diverse life experiences. By being receptive to listening to and understanding the viewpoints of others, you can enhance your own understanding and knowledge of the world. This forms a firm foundation for relationships built on mutual respect and the exchange of ideas.

Exercising Empathy: Openness and curiosity are intertwined with the practice of empathy. Putting yourself in the shoes of others and seeking to understand their experiences and emotions strengthens the bonds of connection. Empathy creates a space where people feel heard, valued, and understood — a quintessential element for building strong and meaningful relationships.

Evince Genuine Interest: Approaching interactions with genuine interest in getting to know people and learning from them creates an environment conducive to forming positive relationships. Asking open-ended questions, listening attentively, and showing interest in others' stories and experiences are ways to cultivate this curious approach.

Cultivating an open and curious approach is essential for attracting healthy and enriching relationships. By delving into the unknown, stepping outside of your comfort zone, and learning from others, you create space for genuine and meaningful connections. This growth-oriented mindset not only enriches your own life, but it also allows you to meet compatible individuals who share your desire to explore the world and build authentic relationships. The open and curious approach extends an invitation to an exciting journey of emotional connection, learning, and personal growth.

The attraction of healthy relationships starts from within. Emitting positive energy, nurturing a positive mindset, practicing authenticity, and being open to new experiences are all essential steps in attracting kindred spirits and building meaningful bonds. Additionally, being prepared to receive love and embracing vulnerability creates fertile ground for deep and enriching relationships. By tending to our own energy and willingness to connect with others, we sow the seeds for a garden of enduring and wholesome relationships.

THE SIGNIFICANCE OF BEING OPEN TO RECEIVING LOVE

While we all crave healthy relationships, we often underestimate the importance of being truly open to receiving love. This involves an introspective journey within, addressing emotional baggage from the past, and nurturing a strong self-esteem.

Profound Self-Understanding

The process of attracting meaningful relationships begins with profound self-understanding. Delving into the depths of one's being is essential in laying solid foundations for significant connections. Here are some ways that profound self-understanding can contribute to the attraction and sustenance of healthy relationships:

Exploring Desires and Needs: Self-awareness encompasses delving into your own desires and needs within a relationship. What values are most important to you? What kind of emotional support do you seek? What are your personal goals and aspirations? Grasping these aspects will help you articulate your expectations clearly and find someone who shares similar objectives.

Identifying Fears and Emotional Wounds: By delving into your fears and emotional wounds, you can avoid perpetuating behavioral patterns that undermined past relationships. This involves taking a look back at past experiences and identifying any traumas or insecurities that might be influencing your current interactions. Awareness of these issues will empower you to approach relationships with greater empathy and understanding.

Breaking Negative Behavior Patterns: Profound self-awareness can help you identify negative behavior patterns that might have marred previous relationships. These patterns might include emotional avoidance, excessive insecurity, trust issues, or other behaviors that hinder the cultivation of healthy relationships. Acknowledging these patterns will enable you to work towards modifying them and adopting more positive behaviors.

Cultivating Self-Esteem and Self-Acceptance: Acquainting yourself with your strengths and embracing your imperfections is essential in attracting healthy relationships. When you have a strong self-esteem and value yourself, you are more likely to attract individuals who also hold you in high esteem. Self-awareness can help you nurture a profound self-acceptance, which is appealing to others and contributes to authentic relationship building.

Articulating Your Needs: Self-awareness also empowers you to communicate your needs effectively in a clear and assertive manner. This is crucial in establishing healthy boundaries and ensuring your emotional needs are met within a relationship. Knowing what you need and being able to express it is a powerful way to attract individuals who are willing to invest in the relationship equally.

Profound self-understanding is a key factor in attracting and sustaining healthy relationships. By delving into your desires, fears, values, and emotional wounds, you gain heightened awareness of your own needs and behavior patterns. This allows for clearer communication, the establishment of healthy boundaries, and the avoidance of negative patterns that could hinder meaningful relationships. Self-awareness is a pathway to personal growth and to attracting relationships that are authentic, rewarding, and founded on mutual respect.

Navigating Emotional Baggage

The emotional remnants of past relationships can become obstacles that hinder our ability to foster and nurture healthy connections. These remnants may include resentments, traumas, distrust, and the fear of becoming vulnerable again. Learning to navigate this emotional baggage is essential in creating space for love and building meaningful relationships. Strategies for managing emotional baggage:

Profound Self-Reflection: Look back on your past relationships and scrutinize the experiences that may have left emotional scars. Identify any grievances, discord, or traumas that may still be coloring your outlook on new relationships. This introspection will help you understand how these experiences have shaped your current beliefs and behaviors.

Acceptance and Forgiveness: Embrace the fact that you carry emotional baggage. Acknowledge the emotions you're holding onto and begin the journey of forgiveness, both for others and for yourself. This does not mean belittling the pain you've experienced; rather, it means choosing to let go of the resentment and anger that may be holding you back emotionally.

Therapy and Professional Support: Sometimes, dealing with emotional baggage can be a daunting task to tackle on your own. Individual therapy or professional counseling can be a valuable tool in navigating through trauma and emotional wounds. A qualified therapist can guide you in safely exploring your emotions and developing strategies to overcome the baggage that is weighing on your relationships.

Personal Development: Investing in your personal growth is a powerful way to manage emotional baggage. This may include reading self-development literature, participating in personal growth workshops, or practicing self-care techniques such as meditation and therapeutic writing. The more you work on understanding yourself and growing as a person, the more proficient you will become at releasing the emotional baggage that may be holding you down.

Open Communication: If you're in a relationship, it's important to candidly communicate your emotional baggage to your partner. This allows your partner to understand your concerns and emotions, which can create space for mutual support and understanding. Open communication can also help to prevent misunderstandings and build trust over time.

Navigating emotional baggage is a challenging but essential process in the journey to attracting and sustaining healthy relationships. By engaging in introspection, acceptance, therapy, personal development, and open communication, you can begin the process of releasing the emotions and beliefs that are holding you back emotionally. As you let go of this baggage, you create space for authentic relationships that are built on love, trust, and mutual understanding. Persistent work on your emotional growth is essential in establishing the foundation for healthy and fulfilling relationships.

Cultivating a Resilient Self-Esteem

Self-esteem plays a pivotal role in attracting healthy and meaningful relationships. When you hold yourself in high regard and cherish your essence, you exude a positive aura that effortlessly draws in individuals who also acknowledge and treasure your virtues. Nurturing a steadfast self-esteem is an ongoing journey of self-discovery, acceptance, and personal growth. Here are some strategies to foster a resilient self-esteem:

Profound Self-Knowledge: To foster a solid self-esteem, delving into profound self-awareness is paramount. This entails exploring your values, passions, talents, and aspirations. The more intimately you get to know yourself, the more adept you become at crafting a self-image rooted in authenticity and self-worth.

Practicing Unconditional Self-Acceptance: Embracing yourself unconditionally is a pivotal step toward nurturing a resilient self-esteem. This involves wholeheartedly embracing all facets of your being, including your imperfections. Acknowledge that perfection is an illusion and that your imperfections are simply part of your growth story.

Commending Strengths: Focus on recognizing and commending your strengths and accomplishments. Make a list of your achievements, both big and small, and revisit these moments whenever self-doubt creeps in. This practice will help you build a positive self-image and reinforce your self-esteem.

Self-Respect and Self-Care: Treat yourself with the same respect and kindness that you would treat a cherished friend. This includes practicing self-care, setting healthy boundaries, and refraining from self-criticism or self-sabotage. The more you treat yourself with reverence, the more others will naturally be inclined to do the same.

Personal Development: Investing in your personal growth is a powerful way to build a resilient self-esteem. This may involve acquiring new skills, pursuing personal interests, and overcoming challenges. The more you challenge and evolve yourself, the more your confidence will grow.

Positive Affirmations: Engage in the daily practice of positive affirmations. These declarations underscore your worth, abilities, and self-acceptance. By repeating affirmations such as "I love and value myself," you are programming your mind to embrace your inherent dignity.

Sidestepping Social Comparison: Constantly measuring yourself against others can erode your self-esteem. Recognize that each individual is a unique being with their own unique path and accomplishments. Focus on your own journey and the traits that make you exceptional.

Cultivating a steadfast self-esteem is essential for attracting healthy and meaningful relationships. As you traverse the realms of self-acceptance, celebrate your strengths, and invest in your personal growth, you will naturally radiate a positive energy that attracts compatible souls. Hold fast to the notion that self-love is the foundation for attracting love from others. The more you cherish yourself, the more adept you will become at attracting relationships that enrich your existence, grounded in mutual respect and genuine admiration.

Releasing Unrealistic Expectations

Being open to receiving love also means being able to let go of unrealistic expectations that can hinder the formation of healthy and meaningful relationships. Often, our vision of a perfect relationship is shaped by external influences such as media, culture, and past experiences. However, these idealized expectations can create barriers to seeing and appreciating the genuine people in our lives. Learning to let go of these expectations and approach relationships with realism is essential for building strong and lasting foundations. Here are some important considerations about unrealistic expectations:

Embrace Imperfection: No one is perfect, including you and your potential partners. It's important to acknowledge that everyone has flaws, vulnerabilities, and moments of difficulty. Embracing imperfection is essential for creating genuine and authentic relationships.

Understand the Complexity of Relationships: Relationships are complex and require ongoing effort from both partners. Releasing the expectation that a relationship will always be easy and free of challenges is essential. Instead, be prepared to face challenges together and work as a team to overcome obstacles.

Value the Authentic Qualities of People: When we let go of unrealistic expectations, we can focus on appreciating the authentic qualities of the people around us. This means recognizing their strengths, talents, and unique attributes. Sometimes, the right person may not fit into all the boxes we've created, but they may possess invaluable qualities.

Communicate Openly and Honestly: Open and honest communication is essential for addressing misguided expectations. Talk to potential partners about your expectations, desires, and concerns. This helps to align both parties' expectations and build a solid foundation of mutual understanding.

Learn from Past Experiences: Past experiences can shape our expectations. However, it's important to remember that each relationship is unique. Use your past experiences as learning opportunities, but avoid generalizing all future situations based on the past.

Focus on Personal Growth: Instead of expecting a relationship to fill all the voids in your life, focus on your personal growth. Develop interests, achieve goals, and work towards self-fulfillment. This not only creates a strong foundation for yourself, but it also makes relationships more complementary rather than dependent.

Releasing unrealistic expectations is essential for attracting healthy and authentic relationships. By freeing yourself from the notion of perfection and embracing the complexity of relationships, you become more open to appreciating people for who they truly are. Open communication, embracing imperfection, and focusing on personal growth are all essential ingredients for building strong relationships where both partners can thrive and support each other. Remember, reality often surpasses expectations, and genuine love thrives when nourished by acceptance, respect, and mutual understanding.

Embracing Vulnerability

Being prepared to receive love means more than just being emotionally available; it also involves being willing to open yourself up and embrace vulnerability. Vulnerability is the cornerstone for building profound, authentic, and meaningful relationships. Opening oneself up to vulnerability is an act of courage that demands authenticity, trust, self-acceptance, and acceptance of others. Here are some important considerations on how to practice vulnerability:

Recognizing and Embracing Your Feelings: Vulnerability begins with acknowledging and embracing your own feelings. This involves being mindful of your emotions and treating yourself kindly, regardless of how uncomfortable those feelings may be.

Sharing with Authenticity: Being vulnerable means sharing your feelings, fears, and desires with authenticity. This doesn't mean revealing every detail of your life, but rather being honest about what you are experiencing internally.

Building Trust Gradually: Vulnerability doesn't have to happen all at once. It's something that can be built gradually as you become more comfortable with the people around you. Start by sharing small aspects of yourself, and as trust grows, delve into more sensitive topics.

Creating Space for Authentic Connections: By allowing yourself to be vulnerable, you are creating a space where others can also open up. This leads to more authentic connections, where both sides can share their experiences and support each other.

Overcoming the Fear of Judgment: One of the biggest challenges of vulnerability is the fear of judgment. It's natural to fear that others might judge or reject you for your emotions and vulnerabilities. However, remember that truly compatible individuals value authenticity and openness.

Fostering Relationship Growth: Vulnerability is fertile ground for relationship growth. When you open up about your experiences and challenges, you allow relationships to evolve beyond the surface. Deep and meaningful discussions help establish lasting connections.

Respecting Your Personal Boundaries: While vulnerability is valuable, it's also important to respect your own personal boundaries. You are not obligated to share more than you feel comfortable with. Vulnerability should be a conscious and respectful choice.

Embracing vulnerability is a pivotal step in attracting healthy and authentic relationships. Through vulnerability, hearts connect, minds understand, and souls touch. Keep in mind that being vulnerable is not a sign of weakness, but rather a display of strength and courage. By allowing yourself to be truly seen and known, you create fertile ground for true and enduring love. Vulnerability not only strengthens relationships, but also enriches your own journey of personal growth.

Attracting healthy relationships is not merely a desire; it's a process that starts from within. By radiating positive energy, nurturing an optimistic mindset, and genuinely being ready to receive love, we become a magnet for gratifying relationships. Recognize that the pursuit of healthy relationships begins with self-love and authenticity, forging a solid foundation for enduring and meaningful connections.

CHAPTER 11

NAVIGATING DISILLUSIONS AND FRESH BEGINNINGS

From disillusions, wings are forged
to elevate your self-love.

Navigating through disillusions and fresh beginnings is a deeply personal and challenging journey. Throughout our lives, we find ourselves confronted with situations where our expectations are thwarted, our hearts are broken, and our lives take an unexpected turn. However, the way we approach these disillusions and fresh starts can make all the difference in our ability to overcome obstacles, grow as individuals, and find a path to renewal. In this chapter, we will delve into strategies for facing disillusions with resilience and embracing fresh beginnings as opportunities for personal growth.

RISING ABOVE THE CONCLUSION OF RELATIONSHIPS IN A CONSTRUCTIVE MANNER

The culmination of a relationship can be one of the most challenging and heart-wrenching experiences one can face. Yet, it is also an opportunity for personal growth, self-discovery, and the creation of a more fulfilling life. Overcoming the conclusion of a relationship constructively involves a series of steps and emotional care:

Embrace the Realm of Emotion

The end of a relationship is a deeply emotional and challenging experience. It's common to experience a complex range of emotions after a breakup, from sadness and pain to anger, confusion, and even relief. Allowing yourself to experience these emotions is a key step in the process of healing and recovery. Why is it so important to allow yourself to feel?

The Validity of Emotions: Every emotion you experience after the end of a relationship is valid and deserves to be acknowledged. It's common to feel guilty for experiencing anger or relief, especially if the relationship was important to you. However, all of these emotions are part of your healing journey and are a natural reaction to a major life change.

Emotional Processing: Allowing yourself to feel helps you process your emotions by allowing them to flow through you. By not repressing or ignoring your emotions, you're allowing them to flow naturally, which may eventually reduce their intensity. Denying or suppressing emotions can prolong the healing process.

Acceptance as the Beginning of Healing: Accepting your emotions is the first step on the road to healing. By acknowledging your emotions, you're honoring your experience and giving yourself compassion during this difficult time. Denying emotions can hinder the healing process and make it more difficult to find renewed emotional equilibrium.

Exploration and Self-Knowledge: By allowing yourself to feel, you can delve deeper into your emotions and what they reveal about your needs, desires, and boundaries. This also offers an opportunity for self-discovery, as your emotional responses can provide insights into areas where you want to grow and empower yourself.

Healthy Expression: Finding healthy ways to express your emotions is essential. This could involve talking to trusted friends, writing in a journal, exercising, meditating, or attending support groups. Constructively expressing emotions can help to reduce emotional tension.

Time and Patience: Navigating the end of a relationship is a process that takes time and patience. Emotions will not disappear overnight, but allowing yourself to feel and gradually confront them can lead you on the path to healing. Be kind to yourself and give yourself the space you need to process what you're going through.

Allowing yourself to feel is a critical step in the journey of dealing with the end of a relationship. Every emotion you experience is valid and deserves to be acknowledged. By acknowledging your emotions, you're starting the healing process and allowing yourself to explore the depths of your feelings, needs, and desires. Recognize that this is a journey, and being willing to experience is a courageous step toward emotional well-being and personal growth.

Seeking Solace

Navigating the end of a relationship is a demanding ordeal that can leave you emotionally overwhelmed. Seeking solace is essential in this juncture, as it offers a tapestry of emotional support, new perspectives, and guidance through the intricate labyrinth of healing. Why is seeking solace so important?

Relinquishing the Emotional Burden: Sharing your emotions with friends, family, therapists, or support groups can alleviate the emotional burden you bear. Talking to people who are willing to listen and offer support can provide a safe space to express your emotions without judgment.

Gleaning Fresh Perspectives: In the quest for solace, you can open yourself up to a variety of viewpoints about your situation. Friends and therapists can offer insights that you may not have considered, helping you to develop a broader perspective on the breakup and a deeper understanding of your own feelings.

Validation and Empathy: When you share your story with people who care about you, they can offer validation and empathy. The feeling of being understood and heard can help to dilute feelings of isolation and loneliness, reminding you that you are not on this journey alone.

Exploring Wholesome Solutions: Those who offer their support can help you to explore healthy ways to cope with the situation. They may offer coping strategies such as relaxation techniques, meditation, exercise, or therapy, all of which can contribute to your emotional healing.

Mitigating Isolation: Seeking solace can also help to combat isolation, which is a common pitfall after the end of a relationship. By connecting with others, you can immerse yourself in a web of social support, an essential pillar in your journey of healing.

Therapy as a Treasured Resource: In addition to the support of friends and family, individual or group therapy can be an invaluable resource. A qualified therapist can provide you with customized tools and strategies for coping with heartbreak and starting over. They can also offer a safe space to explore your deep emotions and work towards personal growth.

Drawing Lessons from Shared Experiences: Participating in support groups or talking to people who have been through similar experiences can offer the opportunity to learn from the experiences of others. Hearing how others have overcome similar challenges can be inspiring and motivating as you embark on your own journey of healing.

The Importance of Self-Compassion: While seeking external support, it is also important to nurture self-compassion. Be kind and patient with yourself, acknowledging that you are going through a difficult time and deserve self-care and self-love.

Seeking solace is an essential part of the process of coping with heartbreak and starting over. Sharing your emotions, gaining new perspectives, receiving validation and empathy, exploring healthy solutions, and mitigating isolation are all valuable rewards of emotional support. With friends, family, therapists, and support groups by your side, the path to healing is made smoother, and your journey towards personal growth is bolstered.

Embrace Self-Nurturance

Navigating the aftermath of a breakup and the beginning of a new chapter following the end of a relationship is an emotionally complex journey. During this time, cultivating self-care is essential, as it serves as a way to protect and strengthen both your physical and emotional well-being. Self-care is more than just a coping mechanism; it is an act of self-love and an investment in your overall well-being. The pivotal role of self-care during this journey:

Wholesome Nourishment: A balanced and nutritious diet has a direct impact on your emotional well-being. Choose nutrient-dense foods that support both your physical and mental health. Avoid excessive amounts of sugar and caffeine, which can potentially impact your mood and energy levels. Remember that making wise dietary choices contributes to emotional balance.

Regular Physical Exercise: Physical activity not only improves your physical fitness, but it also has beneficial effects on your emotional state. Regular exercise releases endorphins, the neurotransmitters of happiness, which can help to reduce stress, anxiety, and depression. Find a physical activity that you enjoy and incorporate it into your daily routine.

Adequate Sleep: Sleep plays a fundamental role in emotional recovery. Make sure to prioritize a sleep routine that allows you to get plenty of restful sleep. Quality sleep not only improves your mood, but it also boosts mental clarity and facilitates sound decision-making.

Activities that Bring You Joy: Engaging in activities that bring you joy and satisfaction is a powerful way to lift your spirits during difficult times. Spend time doing hobbies, spending time in nature, immersing yourself in literature, art, music, or any other pursuit that resonates with your soul. These moments of pleasure can help to reduce stress and brighten your outlook.

Time for Reflection: As you cultivate self-care, make time for reflection and introspection. This could take the form of meditation, journaling, or simply quiet contemplation. The act of introspection can help you to process your emotions, understand your needs, and find clarity in the midst of confusion.

Setting Boundaries: Throughout this period of recovery, it is important to set strong boundaries. This includes setting boundaries with people and situations that may be emotionally draining or harmful. Put your own well-being first, even if that means saying no or withdrawing from certain situations.

Self-Nurturance as Self-Empowerment: The act of practicing self-care is more than just about alleviating suffering; it is an act of empowerment. Taking care of yourself reaffirms your inherent worth and value as an individual. It sends the message that you deserve to devote time and energy to your own well-being, regardless of external circumstances.

Adapting to Change: As you weave the tapestry of self-care, be open to adjusting your approach as needed. Your emotional and physical needs may change over time, so it is important to be flexible with your self-care routine. Stay tuned in to what resonates most deeply with you and make adjustments as needed.

Self-care is an essential compass for navigating the terrain of disillusionment and fresh beginnings following the end of a relationship. A healthy diet, regular exercise, plenty of sleep, pleasurable activities, and moments of reflection all come together in a harmonious symphony that orchestrates your emotional recovery and forges the foundation for the future. Remember that tending to yourself is an act of self-love that rightly deserves primacy in your journey of healing.

Harvest Wisdom from Experience

After the end of a relationship, the journey of recovery involves more than just dealing with the immediate emotions; it also includes the pursuit of profound insights from the experience, which can foster personal growth. Delving into contemplation about the former relationship and its end can help you to plumb the depths of self-awareness. Look within, discerning the tapestry of emotions that were woven during the partnership, the tides of anticipation and need, and the role you played in shaping the overall dynamic. This endeavor is not a quest for blame, but rather a noble exercise in self-understanding.

Discerning Relationship Patterns: By scrutinizing the previous relationship, a discerning eye may uncover patterns of behavior or dynamics that recur across relationships. These may include tendencies to avoid conflict, to prioritize others' needs above one's own, or to seek validation from external sources. Recognizing these patterns is a crucial step towards dismantling undesirable cycles.

Lessons for Future Connections: Ask yourself what wisdom this experience has afforded you. What aspects of positivity do you want to weave into the fabric of future relationships? Which challenges do you need to overcome? Leveraging lessons from the past can help you to steer your compass towards future relationships, fostering intentions that align with a healthier paradigm.

Personal Growth and Empowerment: The transformation of disillusionment into personal growth bestows the mantle of empowerment. Every experience, even the most difficult, can be an opportunity to emerge as a stronger, more self-aware version of yourself. The crucible of learning allows you to recalibrate your internal narrative, focusing on lessons and unearthing your latent potential for growth.

Acceptance and Absolution: The journey of learning from experience dovetails into the realms of acceptance and absolution, embracing both your own being and that of the other party. Forgiveness does not mean condoning what happened; rather, it signifies the emancipation from the emotional burdens that may be sabotaging your equilibrium. This also involves the art of forgiving yourself for past mistakes and embracing the essential truth that all parties involved are fallible, imperfect beings.

Pioneering the Future: Once the process of introspection and learning has taken flight, it is time to look to the future with clarity and intention. Articulate your unique priorities and aspirations for future relationships. Embrace new experiences, yet tether them to the moorings of your values and boundaries as you navigate uncharted relational waters.

Harvesting wisdom from the experience of the past and its conclusion can be a powerful crucible for transforming disillusionment into personal evolution. Identifying recurrent patterns, excavating life lessons, and forging a path towards the future forged with intention are all essential steps on this journey. Each relationship can serve as a nexus of learning and growth, provided you are willing to look inward and commit to your own evolution.

Embrace the Unfoldment

The end of a relationship marks not just the end of an era, but the beginning of a new chapter in your journey. Embracing the unfoldment is a crucial step towards forging a path forward, one marked by vigor and constructive growth. While it's natural to resist change, it's important to allow yourself to experience it, as it can lead to new horizons.

Acknowledging the Pain of Loss: Embracing the unfoldment doesn't mean denying the pain of loss. Instead, it means acknowledging and accepting the range of emotions that come with it, such as sadness, anger, and confusion. These are all natural responses to the end of a relationship. Give yourself permission to feel these emotions without judgment.

Honoring the Tapestry of Memories: Embracing the unfoldment doesn't mean forgetting the memories you shared with your former partner. Instead, it means accepting that these memories are part of your journey and have helped to shape who you are. You can hold these memories dear while still moving forward on your own path.

Letting Go of the Past: Embracing the unfoldment also means letting go of the past. This means letting go of any expectations of how things were or could have been. It means understanding that you are worthy of happiness and growth, regardless of what has happened in the past.

Enfolding the Present and the Future: Embracing the unfoldment also means being present in the moment and open to the possibilities of the future. It's easy to get caught up in the past or worry about what's ahead. But the real power lies in the present moment, where you can make choices that will lead you to your goals.

Unearthing Meaning in Adversity: Change often comes with challenges, but it can also be a source of growth and learning. Within every challenge lies the seed of meaning. Ask yourself what lessons this experience can teach you and how you can grow from it.

Nurturing Resilience: Embracing the unfoldment requires resilience, the ability to adapt to change and overcome challenges. This journey involves developing the emotional and mental strength to face the unknown with confidence.

Welcoming the Unknown: Change often leads us into the unknown, which can be scary. But within the unknown lie hidden treasures. Welcoming the unknown doesn't mean you have to be fearless; it just means facing your fears with courage and curiosity.

Forging a Fresh Narrative: In embracing the unfoldment, you are forging a fresh narrative for your life. This means redefining your values, goals, and sense of self. The power to shape your own story is in your hands.

Embracing the change that comes after the end of a relationship is a journey of self-discovery, growth, and resilience. It involves allowing yourself to feel your emotions, honoring your memories, letting go of the past, embracing the present and future, and unearthing meaning in adversity. Change is an ever-present companion in life, and your ability to embrace it and navigate it will shape your ability to face future challenges with strength and optimism.

Set Boundaries

After the end of a relationship, it is important to establish healthy boundaries to protect your emotional well-being and move forward in a positive way. This exercise in boundary-setting is not just about self-preservation, but also a testament to your self-respect and the respect you have for the other person involved. Here are some important insights on setting boundaries after a breakup:

Define Your Boundaries: The first step is to identify your personal boundaries. What behaviors make you feel comfortable, and what behaviors are not acceptable to you? This could include things like the frequency and type of interactions you have with your ex-partner, or how much personal space you need.

Communicate Your Boundaries: Once you know what your boundaries are, it's important to communicate them to your ex-partner calmly and assertively. Be honest about your needs and how setting boundaries will help you heal and move on.

Take a Break from Contact: Sometimes, it's helpful to take a break from all contact with your ex-partner for a period of time. This gives you both time to process your emotions and adjust to the new dynamics of your relationship.

Disconnect from Social Media: It's also important to disconnect from your ex-partner on social media. Seeing their updates can bring up negative emotions and prolong the healing process. Consider taking a break from social media altogether, or at least unfollowing your ex-partner.

Avoid Triggering Situations: If you know that certain situations or places are likely to trigger negative emotions, avoid them for as long as necessary. This could include social gatherings where you might run into your ex-partner, or places that hold shared memories.

Respect Their Boundaries: It's important to remember that boundary-setting is a two-way street. Just as you deserve to have your boundaries respected, so does your ex-partner. Be mindful of their needs and boundaries as well.

Reassess Your Boundaries Over Time: Your boundaries may change over time as you heal and move on. Be open to reassessing your boundaries as you continue on your journey. What felt necessary at first may no longer be relevant later on.

Prioritize Your Well-Being: Above all, remember that the purpose of setting boundaries is to protect your emotional and mental well-being. Don't feel guilty about creating boundaries that help you heal and move forward.

Setting boundaries after a breakup is an important part of the healing process. By articulating your needs, taking a break from contact, avoiding triggering situations, and respecting the boundaries of others, you can create a healthy environment for yourself to heal and move on.

Avoid Self-Blame

It is common for people to blame themselves after a relationship ends. This may be a way to try to regain some control over the situation or to cope with the pain. However, it is important to remember that relationships are complex, and that both partners play a role in their success or failure. Here are some reasons why it is important to avoid self-blame after a breakup:

Relationships are Dynamic: They are constantly evolving, and both partners influence each other. Blaming yourself entirely for the breakup ignores the other person's role in the relationship.

Breakups are Often Complex: There may be many factors that contributed to the end of the relationship, such as external stressors, differences in values, or unmet needs. It is unfair to blame yourself for everything that went wrong.

Self-Blame Can Damage Your Self-Esteem: It can make you feel worthless and inadequate. Remember that everyone makes mistakes in relationships. Focus on learning from your experiences and growing as a person.

Self-Compassion is Important for Healing: Treat yourself with the same kindness and understanding that you would treat a friend. Forgive yourself for your mistakes and move on.

Acceptance is Key. Accept that the relationship is over and that you cannot change the past. Focus on the present and on building a better future for yourself.

Forgiving Yourself and the Other Person is Important for Closure: Holding on to anger and resentment will only hurt you in the long run. Let go of the past and move on.

By avoiding self-blame, you can focus on healing and moving forward. Remember that you are not alone, and that there are people who care about you and want to help.

Cultivating Patience

The journey of healing after the end of a relationship is a deeply personal and unique one for each individual. Patience plays a profound role in this journey. It is about honoring your own emotions, allowing yourself to move through the different phases of the process, and gradually emerging. Here are some ways to nurture patience during the healing process:

Acknowledge Your Emotions: Allow yourself to experience a wide range of emotions, from sadness and anger to confusion and relief. Don't rush to find comfort. Each emotion is valid and part of the healing process.

Embrace the Stages of Grief: The healing process after a breakup often mirrors the stages of grief: denial, anger, bargaining, sadness, and acceptance. Accept these stages as natural and don't rush through them. Patience allows you to delve deeply into each stage.

Respect Your Own Pace: Everyone heals at their own pace. Don't compare yourself to others. Respect your own personal journey and give yourself the time you need to heal.

Unearth the Significance: During the healing process, you may come to find deeper meaning in the experience. This could include personal growth, a greater understanding of yourself, or even a shift in your life's trajectory.

Celebrate Your Progress: Acknowledge each small step of progress you make. Be proud of yourself when you overcome emotional barriers or embrace new possibilities.

Envision the Future: Be patient as you envision the days ahead. As you heal, you may begin to envision healthy relationships, new experiences, and personal growth. Trust that these things will unfold in their own time.

Cultivating patience throughout the healing process is essential for allowing yourself to heal, flourish, and transform. Honor your emotions, embrace the stages of the process, and be kind to yourself. Patience will not only help you overcome the pain of separation, but it will also guide you towards a brighter future full of possibilities.

EMBRACING NEW BEGINNINGS AND OPPORTUNITIES FOR PERSONAL GROWTH

Although the end of a relationship can be painful, it also opens up a world of new beginnings and opportunities for personal growth. Seizing these opportunities is essential for creating a life full of meaning and fulfillment.

Profound Self-Discovery

The end of a relationship can be a time of profound self-discovery. This challenging phase can be an invitation to explore your identity, passions, and goals at a deeper level. Here are some ways to harness the time after a breakup to get to know yourself better:

Explore Your Interests and Passions: This is a great time to engage in activities that bring you joy. Rekindle interests that may have been neglected during the relationship, or try new things that you've always been curious about. By embracing what you're passionate about, you can reconnect with important parts of yourself.

Contemplate Your Values and Priorities: Take some time to reflect on what's most important to you in life. What are your core values? What are your goals? How do your values influence your choices?

Set Personal Objectives: Use this time to set personal goals that align with your values and passions. These goals could range from learning new skills to achieving personal or professional milestones.

Explore Your Boundaries: The end of a relationship can free you up to explore your emotional, physical, and mental boundaries. What are you comfortable with? What are your limits? Having a clear understanding of your boundaries will help you set healthy expectations for future relationships.

Delve into Your Emotions: Allow yourself to feel your emotions fully. Don't try to bottle them up or ignore them. By exploring your emotions, you can learn more about yourself and what you need.

Practice Self-Compassion: Self-compassion is essential for self-discovery. Be kind and understanding to yourself, just as you would be to a friend. Forgive yourself for your mistakes and accept yourself for who you are.

Learn from Your Past Experiences: The end of a relationship can be a time to reflect on your past relationships and learn from your mistakes. What patterns do you see? What are the things that you want to do differently in the future?

Cultivate Authenticity: As you get to know yourself better, you'll start to develop a stronger sense of your own authenticity. Be true to yourself and don't try to be someone you're not.

Rediscover Your Identity: A breakup can be a time to rediscover your individual identity. Who are you outside of the relationship? What do you want to do with your life? Take some time to explore your interests, passions, and goals.

The time after a relationship breakup can be a time of great personal growth. Use this time to explore yourself and discover what's important to you. This journey will empower you to build healthier and more meaningful relationships in the future.

Set Personal Aspirations

After a breakup, it is important to find ways to move forward and find new purpose in life. One powerful way to do this is to set personal aspirations for your future. These aspirations can serve as a guiding light, helping you stay positive and motivated. Here are some tips for setting and cultivating your personal aspirations:

Do Some Soul-Searching: Before you can set any aspirations, it is important to take some time to reflect on your life and what you want to achieve. What are your strengths and weaknesses? What are your interests and passions? What are your goals for the short-term and long-term?

Set SMART Goals: When setting your aspirations, it is helpful to use the SMART goal framework: Specific, Measurable, Achievable, Relevant, and Time-bound. This will help you to make sure that your goals are realistic and achievable.

Set Multiple Objectives: Don't just focus on one area of your life when setting your aspirations. Consider setting goals for your career, health, relationships, personal growth, and hobbies. This will help you to achieve a more holistic sense of well-being.

Challenge Yourself, but Be Realistic: It is important to set goals that will challenge you, but that are also realistic. If your goals are too easy, you won't feel a sense of accomplishment. But if your goals are too difficult, you may become discouraged and give up.

Create a Plan of Action: Once you have set your aspirations, it is important to create a plan of action for how you will achieve them. This may include setting deadlines, identifying resources, and creating a support system.

Track Your Progress and Celebrate Your Accomplishments: It is important to track your progress towards your aspirations and to celebrate your accomplishments along the way. This will help you to stay motivated and on track.

Be Flexible and Adaptable: Life is unpredictable, and your goals may need to change over time. Be prepared to adapt your goals as needed.

Remember the Journey is Just as Important as the Destination: The journey towards achieving your aspirations is just as important as the destination itself. It is a time of self-discovery, growth, and learning.

Setting personal aspirations after a breakup can be a powerful way to move forward and find new purpose in life. By following these tips, you can set yourself up for success.

Embark on Novel Expeditions

After the end of a relationship, life opens up before you like an expansive landscape of possibilities. This juncture is an ideal moment to explore uncharted waters and embark on new expeditions that may not have crossed your mind before. Embrace this opportunity to broaden your horizons and rekindle the joy of life. Here are some ways to immerse yourself in new experiences:

Engage in Invigorating Pursuits: Take the opportunity to participate in activities that challenge your boundaries and push you beyond your comfort zone. This could include outdoor activities, extreme sports, dance classes, or anything else that piques your curiosity.

Journey and Explore New Frontiers: Travel is an extraordinary way to reconnect with yourself and the world around you. Explore new cities, cultures, and landscapes. In addition to providing new perspectives, travel is a crucible for forging invaluable memories.

Cultivate New Hobbies: This juncture is an ideal time to explore new hobbies or to revisit old interests. Learn to play a musical instrument, dabble in culinary arts, immerse yourself in photography, or pursue any other pursuit that captures your interest.

Participate in Social Gatherings: Engage in social gatherings and events that allow you to meet new people. This could involve workshops, special interest groups, or even virtual meetups. These engagements can help you connect with people who share your passions.

Champion Causes of Consequence: Immersing yourself in volunteer work is a meaningful way to have new experiences while also making a transformative impact on the lives of others. Choose causes that resonate with your values and dedicate your time to making a positive impact.

Acquire Fresh Knowledge: This period provides a perfect opportunity to learn new skills or to delve into subjects that capture your interest. Enroll in courses, workshops, or training sessions that will expand your repertoire and foster personal growth.

Disconnect to Reconnect: Sometimes, the need to detach from digital distractions and the hustle and bustle of everyday life is essential to reconnect with yourself. Participate in meditation retreats, go camping, or simply bask in the serenity of tranquil settings to rejuvenate your being.

Exploring new experiences after the end of a relationship is a powerful way to rediscover yourself and recharge your spirit. Embracing invigorating pursuits, embarking on journeys, nurturing new hobbies, and engaging with new people can not only fill your time but also enrich your life. Seize this juncture to dedicate yourself to personal growth, to evolve personally, and to create lasting memories.

Reinforcing Existing Bonds

After the end of a relationship, it is natural to seek emotional support and a sense of belonging from your existing relationships. Strengthening ties with friends and family members, who may have been neglected during the former relationship, can provide comfort and important reminders that you are not alone on this journey. Here are some ways to strengthen these relationships:

Acknowledge the Importance of Friends and Family: Friends and family are a vital part of your emotional support network. They have a deep understanding of who you are and can often offer invaluable advice and insights. Remember that you don't have to go through this difficult time alone.

Initiate Genuine Contact: The process of reconnecting with friends and family starts with open and honest communication. Be candid about your emotional state and share your feelings openly. By being transparent, you give them a better understanding of your situation and allow them to offer more effective support.

Allocate Quality Time: Schedule time to spend with the people who matter most to you. This could involve deep conversations, enjoyable activities, or simply casual companionship. Quality time helps to strengthen bonds and create positive memories.

Be Open to Receiving Help: Friends and family are often eager to lend a helping hand, but they may not know how best to do so. Be open to receiving assistance, whether it be through conversation, emotional support, or practical help. Allowing them to be a part of your journey can further strengthen these connections.

Navigate Shifts in Dynamics: It's important to recognize that relationship dynamics can change after a breakup. Common friends or family members may find themselves in a difficult position, trying to balance their support for both parties. Be patient and understanding as these dynamics shift.

Prioritize Understanding and Empathy: It's important to acknowledge that everyone has their own unique experiences and perspectives. Make space to listen to and understand the insights offered by your friends and family. Empathy is the foundation for nurturing healthy and supportive relationships.

Treasure the Support You Receive: The emotional support offered by friends and family is invaluable during a time of heartbreak and new beginnings. Cherish those who stand by your side and express gratitude for their unwavering presence and support.

Strengthening existing relationships after a breakup is a meaningful way to secure emotional support and a sense of connection. By reconnecting with friends and family, you not only strengthen those bonds, but you also build a support system that can help you overcome challenges. Remember, you are not on this journey alone, and those who love you will be there to help you face disappointments and embrace new beginnings.

Harvest Wisdom from Missteps

After a breakup, it is natural to reflect on the past relationship and try to learn from the experience. Carefully dissecting the things that went well and the things that didn't can provide invaluable insights that can help you build healthier relationships in the future. Here are a few steps to glean wisdom from past mistakes and relationships:

Candid Reflection: Take some time to engage in honest and unbiased reflection on the past relationship. Think about the good times, but also the challenges and struggles. Avoid getting caught up in the emotional memories, and try to take a broader perspective.

Unearth Patterns: Look for any recurring patterns or behaviors that may have contributed to the end of the relationship. This could involve communication issues, unmet expectations, incompatibilities, or other areas of conflict. The first step to avoiding these pitfalls in future relationships is to recognize them.

Journey Inward: The process of learning from mistakes also involves a deep inward journey. Ask yourself how your own actions, thoughts, and feelings may have influenced the course of the relationship. This may involve evaluating your personal expectations, vulnerabilities, and communication skills.

The Tapestry of Lessons: Discern the pearls of wisdom that can be gleaned from the past relationship. These may include insights into what you value in a partner, behaviors to avoid, more effective communication techniques, and the cultivation of healthy boundaries.

Personal Augmentation: Every relationship, regardless of its outcome, provides an opportunity for personal growth. Reflect on how you can grow from this experience. In what new ways can you approach relationships? How can you become a more evolved version of yourself?

Sidestepping Accusation and Animosity: While it is important to learn from mistakes, it is also important to avoid excessive self-blame or harboring resentment towards the past relationship. Acknowledge the complex tapestry of relationships, where both parties contribute to the dynamic.

Welcoming the Future: By acquiring insights from errors and lessons of the past, you can develop a heightened awareness that will empower you to create thriving relationships in the future. This embrace of personal growth and the application of gained wisdom will enable you to approach new relationships with wisdom and maturity.

The art of gleaning wisdom from mistakes and the tapestry of past relationships is an essential part of the journey of personal growth and evolution. Through the portals of candid introspection, the discernment of patterns, the assimilation of lessons, and the cultivation of self-awareness, you lay the foundation for sturdy edifices of future connections. Understand that each experience, even those that don't meet expectations, kindles a cherished prospect for enlightenment and evolution.

Cultivate Self-Sufficiency

After the end of a romantic relationship, many people find an opportunity to cultivate self-sufficiency and independence. This journey involves mastering the art of contentment within oneself, creating a fulfilling life, and deriving satisfaction from personal achievements. Here are some ways to engender self-sufficiency after the end of a relationship:

Reshape Your Identity: It is common for our identities to become intertwined with those of our partners in relationships. After a breakup, it is important to reconnect with your individuality. What are your passions, interests, and personal goals? This effort is the foundation of your self-sufficiency.

Invest in Self-Enrichment: Dedicate this time to investing in your own growth and development. Learn new skills, pursue your passions, take courses or workshops, and seek out opportunities that challenge you to grow.

Cultivate a Support Network: While self-sufficiency is important, it does not mean isolation. Nurture healthy relationships with friends, family, and colleagues. A strong emotional support network can be essential to your emotional well-being.

Set Personal Milestones: Set goals that are uniquely yours. This could include career aspirations, health goals, hobbies, or any other area of life that is important to you. As you achieve these milestones, you will build a sense of accomplishment that reinforces your self-sufficiency.

Embrace Solitude: Learning to enjoy your own company is an important part of self-sufficiency. Make time for activities that bring you a sense of well-being, whether it's reading, meditating, traveling, or exploring new things.

Prioritize Your Well-Being: Make your physical and emotional well-being a priority. This includes eating a balanced diet, exercising regularly, getting enough sleep, and taking care of your mental health through practices like mindfulness and therapy.

Discover Life's Essence: Develop a deep understanding of what gives your life meaning. This could involve finding purpose in your actions, contributing to your community, or seeking out achievements that bring your personal satisfaction.

Embrace Freedom: Self-sufficiency also means reveling in the freedom that comes with independence. You have the power to make choices that align with your core values and desires, unburdened by constant compromise.

Practice Acceptance: Accept both yourself and your circumstances. Self-sufficiency does not mean denying your emotions or severing connections with others. It means acknowledging your capacity to be whole and content on your own.

Cultivating self-sufficiency after the end of a relationship is a journey of self-discovery and personal growth. Embracing emotional independence, enjoying your own company, and creating a fulfilling life contribute to your overall well-being. This journey can not only enhance your resilience in the face of change, but it can also prepare you to enter future relationships with a solid foundation of self-sufficiency and self-esteem.

Embrace New Relationships with Openness

After navigating the path of coping with disillusionment and new beginnings, being open to new relationships can be a momentous and poignant step on your journey of personal growth. Here are some guidelines to help you embrace this phase of openness and new possibilities:

Renewed Self-Assurance: The process of navigating disillusionment and new beginnings often leads to a renewed sense of self-assurance. As you heal and rediscover yourself, you become more secure in your identity and more attuned to your desires in a relationship. This newfound self-assurance can be a powerful magnet for like-minded people.

Embrace Diverse Experiences: Each relationship is a unique tapestry woven with new experiences and insights. Be open to meeting people from diverse backgrounds, interests, and perspectives. This broader outlook can enrich your horizons and enhance your individuality.

Avoid Comparisons to Prior Relationships: It's natural to draw parallels between new relationships and past experiences, but try to avoid making too many comparisons. Every relationship is a unique opportunity for growth and new beginnings. Constant comparisons can cloud your ability to enjoy the present moment.

Know Your Desires: As you open your heart to new connections, it's important to have a clear understanding of what you're looking for in a partner and relationship. This awareness will empower you to make conscious choices and invest your time in connections that align with your values and aspirations.

Communicate Your Intentions Transparently: When embarking on a new relationship, it's important to be transparent about your intentions and expectations. Communicating your needs and desires from the outset can help avoid misunderstandings and build a strong foundation for the relationship.

Savor the Process of Getting to Know Someone: Getting to know someone deeply takes time and effort. Enjoy this journey of discovery as you learn about their stories, values, and goals. Be open-minded and avoid making snap judgments.

Embrace Uncertainty with Poise: Starting new relationships inevitably involves some uncertainty. Not all relationships will blossom into lifelong romances, but each one can offer valuable insights. Greet uncertainty with resilience and acceptance.

Don't Be Afraid to Take Risks: The fear of being hurt again can be a powerful deterrent to entering new relationships. However, it's important to remember that personal growth often comes from taking calculated risks. Don't let fear hold you back from exploring new avenues of connection.

Continuous Learning: Every relationship, whether successful or not, can teach you something. Reflect on your interactions, assess what worked and what didn't, and use these insights to inform your future choices.

Being open to new relationships is an organic part of the healing and growth process after disillusionment and new beginnings. By embracing this phase with a positive mindset, strong self-assurance, and a willingness to learn, you can create space for enriching experiences, meaningful connections, and the potential to nurture healthy, fulfilling relationships. Remember, each person who enters your life has the potential to teach you something and enrich your journey, regardless of the ultimate outcome.

Coping with disillusionment and starting over after the end of a relationship is undoubtedly challenging, but it also opens up an avenue for personal renewal and growth. The path to success may be difficult, but the journey is inherently rewarding. By facing adversity with resilience, self-awareness, and an optimistic outlook, you can transform pain into empowerment, creating a life that resonates with authenticity, satisfaction, and boundless potential.

CHAPTER 12

CELEBRATING THE JOURNEY OF SELF-LOVE

Celebrate not only the destination,
but also every step, stumble,
and rebirth on the journey
of self-love.

The journey of self-love is a journey of self-discovery, acceptance, and personal growth. Throughout this book, you have explored many facets of this process, mastering the art of nourishing a healthy relationship with yourself. Reaching the end of this path is cause for celebration, as you have taken a momentous step towards a more fulfilling and purposeful life. In this chapter, we will reflect on your evolution throughout the book, discuss how to maintain a focus on self-love even within relationships, and reaffirm that your journey is never-ending and invaluable.

REFLECTING ON YOUR EVOLUTION THOUGHOUT THE BOOK

Look back and reflect on the distance you have traveled since you began this journey. You started out with the intention of cultivating a deeper and more loving relationship with yourself. Now, you have a clearer understanding of how self-love reverberates throughout all areas of your life and how you can surround yourself with it on a daily basis.

Do you remember the times when self-doubt clouded your mind? The times when self-criticism dominated your thoughts? Now, you have the tools to challenge these negative voices and replace them with self-compassion and self-acceptance. You have learned that the journey of self-love is not just about taking care of your physical needs, but also about nurturing your mental, emotional, and spiritual well-being.

Celebrate your accomplishments, no matter how small they may seem. Every step you take towards self-love is a victory. Allow yourself to bask in the pride of your progress and the courage you have shown in facing challenges and transforming negative thought patterns.

MAINTAINING A FOCUS ON SELF-LOVE EVEN WITHIN RELATIONSHIPS

As you move forward on your journey, it is important to keep self-love as a top priority, even when you are in relationships. It is easy to lose yourself in the expectations of others, to give in to their needs, and to inadvertently neglect your own self-care. However, a healthy relationship is built on a foundation of unwavering self-love from both partners.

Recognize that you deserve a relationship that supports and enriches you. This means communicating your needs, setting healthy boundaries, and making sure that your own needs are met. Self-love is the foundation on which you build meaningful and lasting relationships. When you value yourself, you set the standard for how others should treat you.

YOUR JOURNEY OF SELF-LOVE IS NEVER ENDING

It is a continuous path of self-discovery, growth, and evolution. As you overcome challenges, embrace change, and gain deeper insights into yourself, your journey continues to unfold.

Understand that self-love is an ongoing process of learning and practicing. There will be days when you feel deeply connected to yourself, and others when you may feel tested. This is the natural ebb and flow of life. The key is to keep going, even during difficult times.

Celebrating your journey is not just about your past, but also about the promise of your future. You are creating space for a brighter and more conscious tomorrow. As you continue to cultivate self-love, you will discover more about your passions, values, and goals. Your journey is about becoming the best version of yourself, not only for your own benefit, but also for the enrichment of those around you.

As you look to the horizon, recognize that you are worthy of love, happiness, and fulfillment. Your story is unique and valuable, and every step you take is a testament to your commitment to yourself. Celebrate each triumph, each lesson learned, and each revelation unearthed.

Continue to explore, grow, and love yourself. Your journey is a constant reminder that you are the most important person in your life's story. May this celebration of self-love be the beginning of a life filled with love, joy, and authenticity.

CONCLUSION

As we arrive at the culmination of this voyage of self-discovery and self-love, it is paramount to acknowledge the path we have traversed. Throughout this book, we delved profoundly into the multifaceted aspects of the most quintessential relationship of all our relationship with ourselves. Each chapter ushered us into a sojourn of contemplation, growth, and metamorphosis, and I hope you have found both inspiration and guidance to tread the path of self-love.

Unearthing the love of your life transcends romantic entanglements with others. It encapsulates the odyssey of falling in love with who you are, embracing every facet, virtue, and flaw. It encapsulates nurturing a profound and enduring relationship with oneself, erecting a steadfast foundation of self-esteem, self-compassion, and authenticity.

Bear in mind that self-love is not an ultimate destination, but an ongoing trajectory. As we venture forward in life, we encounter challenges, transitions, and novel experiences. However, you now possess all the tools and insights requisite to confront these with both resilience and love for oneself.

Looking back, I hope you can discern the extent of your growth and evolution. Each stride taken toward self-love was an act of valor and self-investment. Celebrate your achievements, however diminutive they may appear, and persist in nurturing the unique relationship you share with yourself.

Recall that the quest for the love of your life is an inner and eternal voyage. Continue to explore, learn, and flourish. Continue to fall in love with who you are, just as you are. And be cognizant that, even amid the most arduous moments, you wield the power to uphold, care for, and unconditionally love yourself.

I extend gratitude for embarking on this journey of self-awareness and self-love alongside me. May the lessons and insights shared within this tome accompany you at every juncture of your path. May you persist in threading a life brimming with love, bolstered by confidence, compassion, and joy.

With love and gratitude,

Leonardo Tavares

ABOUT THE AUTHOR

Leonardo Tavares carries within him not just the baggage of life, but also the wisdom garnered from confronting the tempests it has brought. A widower and devoted father to a charming young girl, he grasped that the journey of existence is a tapestry woven with highs and lows, a symphony of moments shaping our very essence.

With a vibrancy that transcends his youth, Leonardo has confronted challenges, navigated through arduous phases, and faced somber days. Despite pain having been a constant companion along his path, he metamorphosed these experiences into steps that propelled him to attain a plane of serenity and resilience.

The author of remarkable self-help works, including the books "Anxiety, Inc.", "Burnout Survivor", "Confronting the Abyss of Depression", "Discovering the Love of Your Life", "Facing Failure", "Healing the Codependency", "Rising Stronger", "Surviving Grief" and "What is My Purpose?", found in writing the medium to share his life lessons and convey the strength he unearthed within. Through his writing, clear and precise, Leonardo aids his readers in seeking strength, fortitude, and hope in times of profound sorrow.

Assist others by sharing his self-help works.

LEONARDO TAVARES

Discovering
The Love of Your Life